Repositioning for

Marital Success

Your Journey to Marital bliss begins HERE... Be-Located

OBINNA OSITADIMMA OLERIBE

authorHOUSE®

AuthorHouse™
1663 Liberty Drive
Bloomington, IN 47403
www.authorhouse.com
Phone: 833-262-8899

Published by AuthorHouse 07/30/2020

ISBN: 978-1-7283-6807-8 (sc)
ISBN: 978-1-7283-6903-7 (e)

Library of Congress Control Number: 2020914368

Print information available on the last page.

Unless otherwise indicated, all scripture quotations are from
the Holy Bible, King James Version (Authorized Version). First
published in 1611. Quoted from the KJV Classic Reference
Bible, Copyright © 1983 by The Zondervan Corporation.

The Holy Bible, English Standard Version® (ESV®). Copyright
©2001 by Crossway Bibles, a division of Good News
Publishers. Used by permission. All rights reserved.

Young's Literal Translation by. Robert Young, 1862, 1887, 1898.
Author of the Analytical Concordance to the Bible. Revised Edition

Dedicated to

All committed sons and daughters of God who are
waiting and believing God for a change of marital status

CONTENTS

Introduction to Second Edition

I wrote this book while preparing for a seminar for the singles in Tanzania 10 years ago. Since then, I have had several comments and testimonies from the book. People who thought they could not get married, got married; people who were having difficulties in their relationships got repositioned and began to enjoy their relationships; and people who were never asked, "Are you married, will you marry me, etc." became the toast of the city.

As all who got the copies valued the content and wished to have more copies to share, we quickly exhausted the printed copies. I have a leading to print more copies – thus the need for this revised edition.

I have tried to maintain the most of the former content. However, I have also added a few new Chapters based on ten additional years of insight into relationships and marriages.

In this edition, we shall be looking at both the enemies of marital bliss and understanding courtship as separate chapters. I have also added the 9Rs of locating and being located.

Read, enjoy, apply and be blessed.

Obinna Oleribe 2020

+234 803 547 3223

+1541 892 2896

droleribe@yahoo.com;

obinna.oleribe@expertmanagers.org

Before we Begin: Key Question

To our **SISTERS**: If a brother in your church, department, office, unit or group is currently looking for a wife, will you be his first option? Will he think of marrying you – a single, qualified, beautiful, hardworking and tongue speaking sister – praying daily for a life partner? Will he ask for your hand in marriage and give you the opportunity to say either **yes** or **no**?

To our **BROTHERS**: If you were to ask a sister for marriage, will she out-rightly say no to you or take time to think about it? Is there any sister currently praying to God concerning you, asking that God should touch you to propose to her? Are there people going out of their way to win your attention and desire to hear you ask them that singular question…*Will* *you marry me? Do you possess husband qualities that make a sister see you as "Mr Right"*

If your answer(s) (sisters or brothers) to any of these questions is/are no, you are wrongly POSITIONED and so will need re-positioning. And this could be why God has placed this book right now in your hands. This is your season of total turnaround. This is your gateway to marital blessing

Neither great books nor great meetings make great destiny, but great decisions. Until you are re-positioned, you cannot receive your rightful position in destiny. May the grace to make the needed decisions for proper repositioning be granted you right now in Jesus name.

Obinna Ositadimma Oleribe

August, 2010

Acknowledgements

The inspiration to write this book came following a planned singles' seminar in Winners Chapel International (Living Faith Church Worldwide) Dar es Salaam, Tanzania on June 11th – 12th 2010. I therefore wish to acknowledge God for the mandate to write this book, and also:

- Pastor Emmanuel Agi (Regional Overseer East End Africa), Pastor Noel Munuma (Resident Pastor Winners' Chapel International Dar es Salaam), and Pastor Abraham Chilufya (Associate Resident Pastor) for the privilege to labour with them in the vineyard and to be part of the singles' seminar.

- All Assistant Pastors of Winners' Chapel International Dar es Salaam – Pastors Mbata,

Gogomoka, Binamungu, Kapanga, Francis Saliboko, Philip Saliboko, Elinazi and Songolo. Their partnership made my involvement a lot easier.

- All singles of Winners' Chapel International who attended the June 2010 seminar that gave me the opportunity to teach on this topic, and

- My wife, Princess Osita-Oleribe who single handedly edited the first edition, made transforming inputs and made it ready for publication. I am also grateful to Chisom Anukam, Dr Uduak Essen and Adeduro Madeshola for editing and adding values to the second edition of this book.

To you all and my very good friends in Tanzania, I say, asante sana. May my good God and Father bless you all.

Obinna Ositadimma Oleribe

August, 2010

My Testimony

Marriage is a settling phase with responsibility, not a passing phase. It is a journey into a life transforming liberty, but with life-long consequences

I got married in Church on April 28, 2001. Before this day, I had paid dowry on February 18 2001 and had a court wedding on April 12th 2001. Prior to these dates, I scheduled for my traditional wedding for November 25th 2000 and Church wedding for December 2nd 2000, but these days were not to be because of in-law issues.

However, the journey to April 28th 2001 began on June 23rd 1999 when I made a call home attempting to speak to the mother of the house. She was not around. The call was received by her daughter who was so charming on phone that I spoke with her for more than 30 minutes on this first day. Thereafter, I called again and again. This was the days before the advent of GSM in Nigeria. Calls were expensive and phones far in-between. But our God made both phone and time available for these calls.

As the calls became more frequent, I was led to ask her on phone (long before I met her or knew what she looked like) if she would marry me. When she said yes, I got worried for the first time. How can I marry a woman I had not seen, nor met? What if she was not what I expected for a wife? I then requested for her pictures. As she was not a photo freak, she sent the ones she had, and I felt they were ugly! I got more scared.

I made a decision to visit and see her. This was to be a decision-making journey – to continue or to stop. Since I did not know her house, I asked my elder sister to take me to their house. When I entered that early Sunday morning, behold, she was in the living room reading her Bible in a blue night dress. After pleasantries, she took her bath and we all left for church. That day, we worshipped in her church and thereafter we took a walk to see friends and family members. Then we ate in a restaurant and exchanged a number of information. By the end of the trip, I was sure I was on the right track.

We agreed as we continued on our calls to marry in three years from then. However, as our discussions continued and I went to Bible school in August 2000, God asked me to marry. I told her and upon praying, we got a positive nod to move ahead. Although her father opposed the plans initially, God resolved all challenges and we got gloriously married on April 28th 2001.

God went ahead of us. Our first son came exactly nine months after our wedding even when we had not planned for the pregnancy. In fact, we planned against it. But God said, "He shall be the first." Then the second came as a birthday gift to me while I was involved in rural evangelism in a 99 percent Muslim community in Niger state of Nigeria. And then the third both as a conqueror and a worrier called

Winner. We never had to pray for any of them. They came as rewards of the Lord as stated in Psalm 127:3.

Today, we have moved on in several areas of life just because of that major decision – to get married when we did. I give God praise. As I write this book, we are over nine years in marriage. Still young, but we have several testimonies by his grace. And according to the word of His servant on our wedding day, we can stand and testify that our marriage had never seen shame, lack or unfruitfulness. To God be all the glory.

Now it is your turn to testify in Jesus name, Amen.

A note on this Second Edition 2020

We are now 19 years in marriage. Our first son, Alpha is 18 years and still counting. The second will write her West African Senior School Certificate Examination (WASSCE) this year and the third is in JSS3. God has helped us. Our daily prayers on our family altar has strengthened our relationship.

You are next to testify.

PREAMBLE

Let me start this book by stating the obvious. **God loves you**. He so loved you that He sent His only begotten Son to come, live and die for you. And while we were yet sinners, He made that supreme sacrifice. He is concerned with all your problems and challenges, and He is committed to meeting your needs. Your issues are continually before Him.

But the beauty of God is that He is a God of principles and works mostly according to laid down patterns. There is a pattern to find and to be found. This is the main subject of this book.

I am writing this book because of two main reasons. I have over the years had serious compassion for our singles, who despite their commitment to God and His work have not realized their marital destinies. I have joined them in prayers and actually fasted severally for a number of them. Consequently, God revealed to me the answer to the protracted questions of many of our sincere and hardworking singles.

Based on divine revelation; I have found the answer to the questions of many. I believe that with what God has put into my heart, the marital destinies of a number of His children will be fast tracked.

I have also watched good, committed and dedicated Christian sisters and brothers "waste away" while waiting for their marital destinies to be fulfilled. As they waited, time went by and their destinies withered. They waste while their glorious marital destiny is delayed. A good number of them have fasted and prayed uncountable times and believed God strongly for a change of status. Quite a number have attended seminars and workshops on marriages. Some have given offerings, sacrifices and made vows to God, and still nothing seemed to happen. Now a few have even given up, justifying their state by saying, "maybe I am not designed, destined or ordained to get married." But that is a lie of the devil.

The word of life states…*none shall want (lack) her mate*. If God said that *it is not good for a man to be alone*, He knew what He was saying. If he again said that *two are better than one*, He understood the meaning of those words. If He asked that you be *ravished by the love of the wife of your youth* (Isaiah 34:16, Genesis 2:18, Ecclesiastes 4:9, Proverbs 5:18, 19), He designed it for every bona-fide son/daughter of the kingdom. With God, there is no partiality.

The question then is why are there so many unmarried believers in the house of God? Is God unfaithful? God forbids. Let God be true, and all men liars. This burden has been on me for a while and when I began asking God about it, He said to me, "My children are using the wrong keys for their request. Prayer and fasting are not the right keys for marital allocations. There is a place for prayer and fasting. There is a place for offerings and sacrifices, but not in FINDING."

Following divine revelations, I decided to go on a further search on this key to believers' marital allocation. And the product of this search is the basis of this book. I believe that as you read and meditate on the words, that by the end of your studying this book, God would have opened your eyes to the areas of your life that need further attention. As you make the decision to accept the needed changes; your marital destiny will be fully realized.

Great books do not make great destinies, but great decisions and willingness to work them out do. This book will be requiring you to make some fundamental changes in life. Your willingness to make the needed decisions and be committed to following them through is all that is needed to bring you to your superior marital destiny.

I believe God that it will take less than six (6) months from the time of reading and implementing this book for your full marital prosperity to emerge. See you soon in your established homes and families in Jesus name, Amen.

Today, God has deliberately put this book into your hands for two reasons.

- First to bring your period of waiting for your life partner to an end thereby granting you divine access to your own home and children.

- And secondly, to make you a carrier of this new revelation to all singles within and outside your environment. When you must have obtained your testimony, share with others including the secrets that made it come to pass. We have a duty, not only to start and build Godly homes, but also to make sure that all sons and daughters of God have a similar experience of this divine gift called marriage. You shall be the first to testify in Jesus name. Amen.

Unless otherwise stated, all biblical quotes are from King James Version (KJV).

Enjoy the journey into His world of knowledge.

CHAPTER 1

GOD'S DIVINE PLAN FOR EVERY BELIEVER

God would not have created you if He had no plans for you.

You are wonderfully and fearfully made to be

a wonder and to matter to your world.

Luke 1: 18 – 32.

[18]And Zacharias said unto the angel, Whereby shall I know this? for I am an old man, and my wife well stricken in years. [23]And it came to pass, that, as soon as the days of his ministration were accomplished, he departed to his own house.

24And after those days his wife Elisabeth conceived, and hid herself five months, saying, 25Thus hath the Lord dealt with me in the days wherein he looked on me, to take away my reproach among men.

26And in the sixth month the angel Gabriel was sent from God unto a city of Galilee, named Nazareth, 27To a virgin espoused to a man whose name was Joseph, of the house of David; and the virgin's name was Mary. 28And the angel came in unto her, and said, Hail, thou that art highly favoured, the Lord is with thee: blessed art thou among women… 30And the angel said unto her, Fear not, Mary: for thou hast found favour with God. 31And, behold, thou shalt conceive in thy womb, and bring forth a son, and shalt call his name JESUS. 32He shall be great, and shall be called the Son of the Highest: and the Lord God shall give unto him the throne of his father David:

What is God set to do in your life through this book and by the inspiration of the Holy Spirit?

1. **Your kingdom stewardship/services shall be rewarded** (vs. 10 – 18):

God has seen your works in the kingdom and has come down by this encounter to reward you fully for every of those services. You have waited and asked "when will God remember me?" I am here today to tell you without any element of doubt in my mind that God **has remembered** you for good. Your hour of turnaround is now. When God remembers a man, and desires to reward him, He sends an Angel. I am the angel that God is sending your way now concerning your marital destiny. Receive your turnaround blessing right now in Jesus name. Amen.

2. **Your age is irrelevant** (vs. 18):

And Zacharias said unto the angel, Whereby shall I know this? for I am an old man, and my wife well stricken in years.

In the medical world, there is menopause and maybe 'mano' or *'papopause'*. But not with God. Sarah and Abraham had their dream child at a very old age and lived to enjoy it. Job got restored in a very old age and still had the most beautiful daughters in the east (Job 42:12-17). Elizabeth and Zachariah were visited in their old age when Elizabeth was described as well stricken in age. We were not told how old Hannah was when she had Samuel, nor the mother of Samson. With God, therefore, age is immaterial. Only believe.

Also, God restores what was lost. Remember that God restored Ruth with a second husband after the death of her first? What of Abigail? She was also restored and had to Marry David. Even Abraham remarried after Sarah's death and had children. So, peradventure you have lost your first spouse and you are still less than 60 years, there is hope for you. New God ordained relationship is possible and likely. Believe it.

3. **You are coming out of your hidden positions** (vs. 24):

And after those days his wife Elisabeth conceived, and hid herself five months, saying,...

Elizabeth was married for so long (Bible did not tell us how long). But we know that it was for a long time because Bible records that the visitation of the angel was in their old age. She conceived at that advanced age, and what looked impossible became possible. As a reward to her husband's kingdom stewardship, she conceived. There is always something that must come before the 'after these things' experience. She conceived and for 5 months, hid herself as she was not sure what people would say – mock or laugh with her?

You may be hiding too from your family members, friends, peers, etc. You are tired of answering their probing questions on why you are not married yet. You are tired of their mocking, jesting and insults.

Relax, your months and years of hiding are coming to an end. And I declare, according to the word of God, "After this book, your situation will change."

4. **Your marital reproach shall be rolled away** (vs. 25):

Thus hath the Lord dealt with me in the days wherein he looked on me, to take away my reproach among men.

She was married and barren, but her barrenness was removed and she conceived. God deals with people in different ways. Elizabeth confessed that, so has God dealt with her.

God will be dealing with you through this book; and by the end of this journey, you will emerge victorious, laughing and smiling because all your life reproaches would have been rolled away. Truly, you will confess that the lines have fallen unto you in pleasant places – that you now have a goodly heritage.

5. **You shall in the next 21 days receive angelic visitation** (vs. 26):

And in the sixth month the angel Gabriel was sent from God unto a city of Galilee, named Nazareth

Angelic visitation is still very real and for you, your visitation is imminent. God is sending your way within the next 21 days, your Angel of change. Just like Gabriel visited Mary in the sixth month, God is sending your own angel now. Be expectant as expectation is the mother of all manifestations. You do not experience what you do not expect.

So, as you go through this book, be full of expectations that God will not only mention your issues, but will also send help your way.

6. **You shall be espoused to your spouse – wife or husband** (vs. 27):

To a virgin espoused to a man whose name was Joseph, of the house of David; and the virgin's name was Mary.

There is a God-ordained wife or husband for you. Be not deceived, for "faithful is He that calleth you, who also will do it (1Thess5:24). Before He formed you in your mother's womb, He had already completed your glorious marital destiny. That is why He will authoritatively say, *none shall want (lack) her mate.*

God does not need to create another person right now before you could marry. Your destiny-ordained partner is just around the corner. Do you believe your spouse is actually looking for you now? Yes, they have lost their sleep and peace. They are closer to you than you will ever imagine. By the end of this journey, God would have opened your eyes to how you can locate him or her.

7. **You shall be highly favoured** (vs. 28):

And the angel came in unto her, and said, Hail, thou that art highly favoured, the Lord is with thee: blessed art thou among women

It is the favour of God that flavors the destinies of men. God is set to favour you beyond your dreams for He is able to do exceedingly, abundantly above all you can ever ask, think or imagine.

In His favour is life – including marital life and I see you receiving it right now in Jesus name. Favour is what it takes to end the struggles of life. Favour wipes away shame and reproach. Favour changes status and gives a new beginning. Favour brings to an end labours of life…including marital labour. You will enjoy the favour of God.

But, just like natural favour, divine favour is not FREE? There is a basic spiritual requirement to receive it. First, you must be righteous… the Word says in Psalm 5:12,

"For thou, LORD, wilt bless the righteous; with favour wilt thou compass him as with a shield."

Righteousness (which is not self-righteousness, but righteousness purchased by the finished work of Christ on the cross) is your qualification for divine favour, and kingdom service is your access. Hear what the Word says again from Psalm 102: 13-15 says:

"Thou shalt arise, and have mercy upon Zion: for the time to favour her, yea, the set time, is come. 14For thy servants take pleasure in her stones, and favour the dust thereof. 15So the heathen shall fear the name of the LORD, and all the kings of the earth thy glory."

Kingdom service qualified Zacharia for God's intervention and favour, I see you enjoy the fullness of His favour through service and righteousness.

8. **Fear shall be destroyed:** (vs. 30)

And the angel said unto her, Fear not, Mary: for thou hast found favour with God.

Fear (False Evidences Appearing Real) is of the devil. A number of you are where you are today because of several fears – fear of disappointments, fear of making the wrong decisions, fear of moving away from the program of God for your life; fear based on ugly past experiences, history of parental marital challenges, and other negative reports from the camp of the enemy. God, by this book in your hand, is destroying all roots of fear and setting your destiny free to blossom.

Why again should fear be destroyed? Fear is the opposite of faith. Without faith, you cannot please

God. Even the devil knows that unless God is happy with you, He cannot work out your destiny. He, therefore, brings fear to keep you alienated from God. But his devices have been laid bare and from today, you shall work in faith and not fear. Let this be your foundation – marriage is good because God said so (Gen 2:18).

9. **Once married, you shall conceive and bring forth a child that shall be great and glorious** (vs. 31 – 32).

And, behold, thou shalt conceive in thy womb, and bring forth a son, and shalt call his name JESUS. [32] He shall be great, and shall be called the Son of the Highest: and the Lord God shall give unto him the throne of his father David…

This is God's plan for you and even the devil knows and cannot do anything about it. To stop it, devil has over the past few years, worked at delaying your blessings. But he has failed already.

He knows that the seeds that will come from you shall be great, sons/daughters of God; and able to trample him under their feet. But from today, his hold is destroyed in Jesus name, Amen.

Are you set for an encounter with GOD? Bow down your head right now and ask for whatever you want from God from this book. Any of the nine levels of blessings is available for you. You only need to ask. I join my faith with yours and speak into your life right now. Receive your heart desires in Jesus marvelous name, Amen.

Marriage is a great gift from God to man. God is the author of marriage. He is the vital third party in the marriage covenant. Man cannot truly marry in God's own way without His involvement.

Marriage is good and wonderful. Just as everything from God is good. There are seven fundamental principles of marriage. I will in the next chapter briefly speak on these fundamentals of marriage.

If you are married and want to keep enjoying your marriage, read my books on Celebrating Marital Success. I have other books on Making Maximum Impact, Scaling New Heights and Transforming Ideas into Entrepreneur and Greatness.

Find any or all these books to scale new heights in marriage.

CHAPTER 2

FUNDAMENTALS OF MARRIAGE

*Ignorance of foundational principles makes decay and
decadence inevitable. It is the depth of a foundation
that determines the height of a building*

Genesis 2:18-25

*¹⁸And the LORD God said, It is not good that the man
should be alone; I will make him an help meet for him.
²¹And the LORD God caused a deep sleep to fall upon
Adam, and he slept: and he took one of his ribs, and
closed up the flesh instead thereof; ²²And the rib, which
the LORD God had taken from man, made he a woman,
and brought her unto the man.*

²³And Adam said, This is now bone of my bones, and flesh of my flesh: she shall be called Woman, because she was taken out of Man. ²⁴Therefore shall a man leave his father and his mother, and shall cleave unto his wife: and they shall be one flesh.

²⁵And they were both naked, the man and his wife, and were not ashamed.

This was the mandate that began marriage. God created the whole earth in Genesis Chapter 1 and blessed man. He commanded man to reproduce and replenish the earth. However, to achieve that mandate, unknown to man, man needed a help meet – woman. God knowing this, therefore, began a new creative process that culminated in marriage. What are the key lessons from this process in Genesis Chapter 2?

1. **Marriage is fundamentally God's idea** (Vs 18):

And the LORD God said, It is not good that the man should be alone; I will make him an help meet for him.

Man had no single input to the idea of marriage. God decided that man should not be left alone because according to Him, it was not good. Therefore, marriage is not a social or cultural thing – it is a God thing!

Attempting to marry outside God is recipe for trouble. No wonder several marriages today are failing. The natural man does not have what it takes to make a marriage work – no matter how much they try. It takes God. To have a good home and family, God must be the foundation. *For, "If the foundation be destroyed, what can the righteous do?"* (Ps 11:3). God is the right foundation of every true and prosperous marriage. While many plan wedding days, very few plan for the life-long marriage. It takes God to make it work.

Marriage is not a traditional or cultural thing. It is a godly thing. Marriage is not designed by God to fulfill all righteousness, but to make your life more fulfilling. It is not a burden to be endured, but a blessing to enjoy. Moreover, marriage is not covenanted at the village square but in His presence. That is why Mathew 22:2 – 3 said:

The kingdom of heaven is like unto a certain king, which made a marriage for his son, ³And sent forth his servants to call them that were bidden to the wedding…

Till date, God is still putting marriages together. He will put yours together sooner than you expect. How? It does not take time. It only takes God. He did it for me. He will do it for you.

I was working in Abuja and wanted to use my savings to buy a car. But I heard God say to me, "Marry first." I assume that the money I had was, therefore, designed to be used for the process. So, I began, but one parental challenge made me spend all the funds without getting married. Then, God stepped in. Once all roads were cleared for our marriage, God provided everything including free reception hall, chairs and drinks, free accommodation for all guests from outside Abuja, free vehicles for all movements and above all stress-free wedding and marriage since April 28th 2001. He that did mine will also do yours in Jesus name. Amen.

2. **Marriage is Good:** The above verse of the scriptures makes it clear that it is not good for a man to be alone. In other words, it is good to be married! Irrespective of what you have experienced in life, irrespective of what your parents or grandparents may have gone through, and irrespective of what your friends and family members maybe going through right now, I have come with this good news: **marriage is good**.

I have tested the goodness of marriage. When we were getting married, the Bishop at our local church in Abuja came in miraculously (he rarely officiated in weddings). On that day, when I saw his seat empty, I prayed a silent prayer telling God that the seat will not remain empty all through the wedding ceremony. Just before the end of the ceremony, he walked into the church and took over the microphone to bless us. He said, "This marriage will not see shame. This marriage will not borrow. And this marriage will be fruitful." Our marriage has enjoyed these three dimensions of blessings over and over again. When we married, we had no car; all the cars used were from the office where I worked or friends. But by His grace, we have given out cars as gifts. Buy His grace, buying cars is no longer a prayer item. When we married, we were tenants, but God has built us houses and is willing to build more. Our annual gross income then was much less than our monthly net income today. Truly, we have not borrowed.

We wanted to start having our children three years post marriage, but God said; "your seed shall be the first". We were eleven couples that got married on the same day, a number got pregnant before my wife. But our son, Alpha, came three weeks earlier than his EDD at 4.1 kg to fulfill His promise – your seed shall be the first. Since then, we have had two other children – Delight and Winner – all without praying. Why? Marriage is good. Delight came as a birthday gift while Winner appeared as a reward of service. Truly marriage is good.

For over 19 years today, I am yet to raise my voice on my wife. God has made us a reference point of His goodness. Why? Because marriage is good! I am convinced that for you who is reading this book now; your marriage will be even better and sweeter in Jesus name.

When we got married, offerings were in hundreds of naira. But today, if I give anything less than multiplies of four figures in Nigerian currency as an offering, I will be insulting my God. My tithes today are far greater than my annual income when I got married some years ago. Why? Marriage is good. God is a God of good gifts.

As I write this segment, I just remembered that I have had better visas where I was previously refused, have had jobs in foreign currency, got my doctorate at a record-breaking time, and I have never had need to borrow anything from anyone because **"marriage is good."**

- Good is actually God plus zero (emptiness, nothing). **GOD + O = GOOD.** In order words, God transforms your emptiness, nothingness and zeros into good; God specialized in adding O - other blessings into our lives and one of the ways through which He adds is by marriage.

- But evil is Devil minus D. DEVIL – D (decoration) = EVIL. This emphasizes the fact that Satan subtracts divine decorations from people.

Walking and working, therefore, with God adds other blessings to our lives and destinies. He will add to yours now and always.

To re-emphasis the goodness of marriage, God said in Ecclesiastes 4:9 - 12: Two are better than one…. and a three-fold cord cannot be easily broken. Nothing shall be able to break you in Jesus name.

3. **Marriage has a purpose:** (Vs 24)

   THEREFORE shall a man leave his father and his mother, and shall cleave unto his wife: and they shall be one flesh.

   To every marriage, there is a '**therefore**'. This in some translations is translated as "For this purpose…", "For this cause…" (See Matthew19:5, Mark10:7 and Eph5:31). There is always a purpose for marriage.

Men may have their reasons or purpose, but God has the ultimate purpose.

He said that it was not good for a man to be alone and therefore, a help meet was needed. The primary reason therefore for every God ordained marriage is not to have babies (although this is good and part of the covenant), to have more output and to become wealthy (although this also is part of it as two shall put ten thousand to flight Deuteronomy32:30), but for COMPANIONSHIP. God believes in fellowships and companionships. This is therefore the primary reason He gave us wives/husbands that we be not alone. Other benefits of marriage are primarily all manner of additions as we see in Matthew6:33.

What does the Bible say about this? Let us look at the book of Ecclesiastes 4:9-12 which we mentioned earlier:

***Two are better than one; because they have a good
reward for their labour. ¹⁰For if they fall, the one
will lift up his fellow: but woe to him that is alone
when he falleth; for he hath not another to help
him up. ¹¹Again, if two lie together, then they
have heat: but how can one be warm alone? ¹²And
if one prevail against him, two shall withstand
him; and a threefold cord is not quickly broken.***

Did you hear it? Two are better than one because
they have a good reward for their labour. I see God
planting you in your own God ordained home in
Jesus name, Amen.

It was companionship that made me ask my
beautiful wife to leave her well-paying job in
Nigeria to join me in Tanzania when God sent me
here for a task. Although I had an international
appointment, I saw my job as a visa to serve God in
a new dimension in East Africa. When I asked her
to leave her work, there were no deliberations, she

just obeyed and joined. Companionship to us is far more than the monthly income of four-dollar digits she was making. We made the decision also to move with our children because building a godly home is our primary responsibility.

4. **Marriage is for men and women** (Vs 24). Marriage is not for boys and girls

   Therefore shall a MAN leave his father and his mother, and shall cleave unto his wife: and they shall be one flesh.

   Being a man speaks to maturity. Maturity, however, must be in four dimensions – physical, mental/psychological, economic, and spiritual.

   Physical maturity talks about age. Marriage is not for the infants. Medically speaking, there is an age a boy or girl cannot and should not marry. This is because, their bodies are still in the process of development and marrying and having babies at this stage can destroy their lives and wellbeing. This is the major cause of injuries in the birth canals of young girls as they deliver – called versico-vaginal fistula (VVF). When this happens, urine and sometimes faeces begin to leak from their private part. Victims of this problem smell; wear pads at all times and may lose their spouses. Moreover, the children of such pregnancies hardly survive. Developing men may be physically unable to handle the marital responsibilities. So, marriage is for the physically matured.

Mental or psychological maturity is the next dimension of manhood. This involves acceptance of responsibilities and financial independence. Marriage is a project with cost, time and quality implications and constraints. To enjoy the benefits of marriage, the couple must be willing to accept responsibilities for their actions, decisions and even inactions. The man must be mature enough to cater for somebody else, look beyond self, share resources with wife and extended family members as the need arises. He should also be able to handle emergencies and pay family related bills. A mentally matured man must have his own place, pay his bills, make his decisions and believe God for best outcomes. He must also be mentally accommodating, able to sit down and plan his finances (Mat 14:28) before marriage, be caring, trusting and understanding.

This also means he/she must be economically matured with a dependable income stream to meet the financial needs of the family.

As marriage is of and from God, spiritual maturity is vital and crucial to successful marriages. Having a well-established work and walk with God is fundamental. This is not necessarily how long, but how deep. Many novices in the kingdom have made shipwrecks of their marriages because of shallow walk with God.

I got married to my wife as a young Christian, but I was deep. I gave my life to God less than a year earlier. But then I went to Bible school where I was totally transformed and even had a change of name. It was also while in the Bible school that God spoke to me on a number of issues. Many are counting the number of years they have worked and walked with God. This is good. But God is more interested in how deep you are with Him. Spiritual maturity refers to your depth in God.

I have said it before and I will say it again: Love for each other is never enough and does not guarantee successful marriage. Therefore, do not marry a man or woman that just loves you; marry somebody that loves God and is willing to get to higher heights and greater depths in God. I will dwell on this later in this book. You will find your own in Jesus name.

5. **Marriage involves leaving and cleaving:**

> *Therefore shall a man LEAVE his father and his mother, and shall CLEAVE unto his wife: and they shall be one flesh.*

Until you leave, you cannot cleave. "Cleave" demands C-Leave, meaning Complete leave. For leaving to be complete, it must also occur in the four dimensions – physical, mental, economic and spiritual.

I see leaving as complete separation from one's family of birth or orientation. For instance, you have not left if you are still living in your parents' house. Even if they offered you an opportunity to stay back and live with them, refuse! New couples need free time to get to know each other, learn themselves without interruptions, handle their challenges and successes, enjoy each other, and develop love for each other's company. Living with family members limits this process. That is why, a newly wedded couple is advised to stay alone for some months to years before allowing family and friends to come and live with them.

If your parents are still making decisions for you, you have not mentally left. If at every small issue, you run back to your parents for their opinions, guidance and counseling, you have not mentally left. A mature man makes his own decisions and takes responsibility for them. In our marriage, I have this testimony that I have never gone to any of our parents (biological or in-laws) for support in any challenge or help in decision making process.

They are only informed of decisions we have made. We only informed them when we gave out our car; we only informed them when we finished our houses. Some actually knew of them for the first time when we invited them over. We only informed them when we had our babies; we only informed them when we decided we were leaving for East Africa, etc. They only get information – they have never helped us make family related decisions. Why? …Because we left them a long time ago. Before you marry therefore, understand that you have to leave to effectively cleave.

If your parents are still funding your necessities, you have not left economically. If mum has to go to market for your family once in a while, if you have to go 'home to collect food stuffs' once in a while, if you are on parental salary monthly, you are still their baby and not a man or woman yet. Leave economically.

If you are also in church just because that is where your parents' worship, you have not spiritually left. I have heard a number of people say that they cannot leave because if they do, their parents will not be happy. Am I saying that you should not make your parents happy? No. All I am saying is that you do not mortgage your destiny because of spiritual slavery. A number of born-again Christians have had to buy cigarette and alcohol, indulge in questionable rituals during their weddings to satisfy the wishes of their parents and sponsors. Some in a bid to make their parents happy; have had their marriages blessed by people that had no good marriage testimonies, yet expected marital testimonies. No one can give what he does not have. Wake up! Life is a journey. Everyone is on his own track. Success or failure in life and marriage is an individual thing. Brace up. Take responsibility.

I remember when I was to marry, and I was asked to come back home and wed at home. I cleverly refused. I sent a message home telling everybody that I needed to be blessed by my Bishop as I will continue and build my home under him. I actually told everyone to come if they could come on their own, and they came. When I was paying the dowry, I was asked to buy alcohol and cigarette. But I refused. When my in-laws insisted and quoted, "Give unto Caeser the things that are for Caeser's and to God the things that are for God", I responded by telling them that I would rather, "Do unto others as I would like them do unto me." How I wish it was now that I know more of the scriptures? I would have asked them to show me their inscriptions on the bottles of beer or packets of cigarette.

You need spiritual maturity if you want to have a good home. Two of the major benefits of maturity before marriage is ability to handle challenges (because they will come!) and free access to God's wisdom bank (a major requirement for building a good home).

Now to cleaving in Biblical sense: This means joining, sticking together just like with a gum. Try separating two books that were joined. What happens? It gets torn. That is why God said "He hates putting away (Malachi 2:14-16).

Divorce destroys lives and people. It always has negative impacts on the people involved. I believe the only allowable reason for separation is death. However, only the mentally /psychologically matured can effectively cleave.

1. **Marriage leads to the birth of new person(s):**

   Therefore shall a man leave his father and his mother, and shall cleave unto his wife: and THEY SHALL BE ONE FLESH.

   In marriage, the two become one – your old self (the bachelors and spinster) dies, and a new you – the married person – emerges. This is just like in the four-stage metamorphosis of insects; there is a complete change from egg to larva and from larva to pupa and from pupa to adult. At marriage, you transform from egg unto larva. I know you will be asking; when do I become a pupa or an adult? Pupa stage is the pregnancy stage, and adult is the parenthood period.

These are similar, but there are great transformations at each of these stages. By this analogy you will discover that a woman goes through several pupa stages based on the number of children planned for. Why? Each pregnancy is unique and has its own characteristics.

Understanding this metamorphosis helps couples to adjust to the changes. The Bible says that both become one. ...One in what? ...In vision, in planning, in goals, in decision making, in handling challenges and in managing resources. When this oneness is not achieved, marital challenges emerge.

2. **Marriage thrives on trust and openness** (Vs 25):

   And they were both NAKED, the man and his wife, and were not ASHAMED.

   Unless there is total trust and openness, marriage vows will fail. I said earlier that in marriage, love for each other is not enough. You need openness to totally enjoy your marital destiny. ...Openness in what?

   a. In your finances – sources, how much, where they are kept and how they are used.

   b. In your relationships – past, present and if possible, future.

   c. In career decisions – and their impacts on the family; etc.

The basic seed of openness is **trust**. Once there is full trust and understanding, openness will thrive. But where trust is lacking, openness is impossible. How much of your spouse you know is dependent on their levels of openness between you both. If your spouse is always suspecting your words, trips or discussions and every telephone call you make or text messages you send, then the relationship lacks trust. If upon your return from a trip, your spouse begins to search your materials for evidence of wrong doings, there is neither trust nor openness. Marriage thrives on trust and openness

Openness begins in courtship. How many children do you intend to have? Are you going to have individual or joint bank accounts? Which church will you attend after marriage? In which city will you live? What is your career path in life? These must be extensively discussed if openness must be realized. If, however, an inevitable need arises for a change in initial plans; these must be discussed and understood by both parties, and agreed upon. Also discuss past relationships, past mistakes and life turning points. Discoveries from these open discussions will lead to a better relationship in future. In some circumstances, it may lead to broken courtship. Remember, however, that broken courtship is a blessing, but divorce is a curse.

Couples bond better when they truly know each other. We travel a lot individually, but trust in our relationship is unshakable. As I began to write this book, I received a call and it was for a training appointment with a bank running into millions. She knew about it when I applied for it. I did not need to wait until I got home to tell her, I told her during our very next call while still in office. What are you hiding? That maybe what is or will destroy your marriage. Be open!

Openness saves you the headaches of wondering what you have shared and what you have not shared. Truth preserves openness. Purpose from now to be open and you will reap the benefits thereof. Amen.

4. **Marriage is a work:**

Let me end this section with this: marriage is a **W.O.R.K**. The home is not a playground, but a workplace. For instance, it is a work to find your life partner, it is a work to plan the marriage process, it is work to have and train children, and it is a great work to generate the goodness in marriage. Each of these work levels has their challenges, cost, quality expectations, and requirements.

Wherefore, my beloved, as ye have always obeyed, not as in my presence only, but now much more in my absence, work out your own salvation*(marriage)* ***with fear and trembling*** (Philippians 2:12).

Hebrews 3:4 says: ***"For every house is builded by some man; but the builder of all things is God."*** You need to build your house. You need to work out the salvation of your house with fear and trembling. It is your responsibility. That is why you must realize that

- Marriage is of and from God, and therefore make God the unseen Guest in every meal and discussions.
- Marriage is good and being committed is needed to enjoy the goodness that it brings.
- Marriage has a purpose and work always to achieve that purpose.

- Marriage is for the matured minds – physically, mentally, economically, and spiritually; and therefore, build up yourself in whichever way you know you are deficient.

- Marriage involves leaving and cleaving, therefore be willing to leave – body, soul and spirit – and cleave to your spouse in good and not so good times.

- Marriage requires the development of a completely new you and therefore allow change and adapt to good changes; and finally,

- Openness is the cement of good marital destiny.

What again is work in the context of a marriage?

W – Wisdom. Bible says that through wisdom is a house built and by understanding it is established. Ask God for wisdom to build your home.

O – Openness. And they were both naked and not ashamed. Openness destroys shame and reproach in marriages. Strive for total, not partial openness.

R – Responsibility. Every house is built by some man, but the builder of all things is God. Accept responsibility. Take full responsibility for your family's success and work at it.

K – Kneel. The effectual and fervent prayer of the righteous makes tremendous power available. Kneel regularly on behalf of your family. It is God that truly unites, develops and makes things beautiful. Develop a functional and spiritually guided prayer life. Be sensitive in the spirit and continuously stand in the gap for your family. God is waiting for your prayers.

Now that you completely understand the fundamentals of marriage, in the next chapter, I will be spending the next few pages to speak on the first level of work in marriage – finding a life partner. Ready

CHAPTER 3

BASIC TRUTH IN FINDING A LIFE PARTNER

You shall know the truth and the truth shall set you free. But the truth that sets free is not free. Therefore, buy the truth and sell it not...Buy and adhere to the truth

Truth No 1: CHANGE is a MUST:

Romans 12: 1-2

I beseech you therefore, brethren, by the mercies of God, that ye present your bodies a living sacrifice, holy, acceptable unto God, which is your reasonable service.

²And be not conformed to this world: but be ye transformed by the renewing of your mind, that ye may prove what is that good, and acceptable, and perfect, will of God.

There is one thing in life that is as constant as life itself: CHANGE. Things are always changing around us and in us. The world is programmed to change – howbeit *negatively*. The world is in a continuous random motion that brings about negative changes – fruits get bad, houses decay, unwashed cloths and bodies smell, etc. Negative changes therefore occur regularly in a passive manner, but positive changes must be actively orchestrated to manifest.

We change our dresses, our locations, our cars, our friends, our jobs, film preferences, etc. It takes quality decision to live a decent life, quality determination to live a sanctified life, and quality dedication to succeed in life and ministry. Positive changes are programmed, planned and deliberately made to happen.

I know that change is inevitable to actualize what I am about to tell you in this chapter. This is the main reason for writing this book. I acknowledge that positive changes sometimes are hard, but they are not impossible. Every believer has a superior partner who can help actualize the positive CHANGE process. He is called the Holy Spirit. You need this power for true and lasting change.

Isaiah 32:15 expressly says:

Until the spirit be poured upon us from on high, and the wilderness be a fruitful field, and the fruitful field be counted for a forest.

Psalm 104: 30 says:

Thou sendest forth thy spirit, they are created: and thou renewest the face of the earth.

It takes the Holy Spirit to turn a barren life (wilderness) into a fruitful field and then unto a forest. It takes the Holy Spirit to renew a life and destiny, and to create something new. You can depend on Him to do a work in you that will take you to a height you never imagined. Receive the empowerment of the Holy Spirit right now in Jesus name. Amen

Second you need guidance: Romans 8:14 says:

For as many as are led by the Spirit of God, they are the sons of God.

You need the guidance of the Spirit to know what to do per time, what changes to implement, and what track to follow. The Psalmist said that the steps of the righteous are ordered of the LORD (Ps 37:23). I see God ordering your steps in Jesus name.

Truth No 2: MARRIAGE is for ALL

Let us now establish another simple Biblical truth. Who should marry? The answer to this question is found in Isaiah 34:16 which says:

Seek ye out of the book of the LORD, and read: no one of these shall fail, NONE SHALL WANT HER MATE:

for my mouth it hath commanded, and his spirit it hath gathered them.

When God says, 'none', He means 'none'. None shall lack or want her mate. That means there is a partner for everyone somewhere all the time.

Why should all marry? For six main reasons:

1. Two are better than one: Ecclesiastes 4:9-12:

    Two are better than one; because they have a good reward for their labour. ¹⁰For if they fall, the one will lift up his fellow: but woe to him that is alone when he falleth; for he hath not another to help him up. ¹¹Again, if two lie together, then they have heat: but how can one be warm alone? ¹²And if one prevail against him, two shall withstand him; and a threefold cord is not quickly broken.

2. To enjoy the blessings of your father – romance: Proverbs 5:15-20

> *Drink waters out of thine own cistern, and running waters out of thine own well. {16}Let thy fountains be dispersed abroad, and rivers of waters in the streets. {17}Let them be only thine own, and not strangers' with thee. {18}Let thy fountain be blessed: and rejoice with the wife of thy youth. {19}Let her be as the loving hind and pleasant roe; let her breasts satisfy thee at all times; and be thou ravished always with her love. {20}And why wilt thou, my son, be ravished with a strange woman, and embrace the bosom of a stranger?*

3. To make greater impact in life and ministry: Hear what Deuteronomy 32:30 says,

> *How should one chase a thousand, and two put ten thousand to flight, except their Rock had sold them, and the LORD had shut them up?*

4. To have godly seeds (Children, the reward of the Lord). Malachi 2:14-15:

Yet ye say, Wherefore? Because the LORD hath been witness between thee and the wife of thy youth, against whom thou hast dealt treacherously: yet is she thy companion, and the wife of thy covenant. [15]And did not he make one? Yet had he the residue of the spirit. And wherefore one? That he might SEEK A GODLY SEED. Therefore take heed to your spirit, and let none deal treacherously against the wife of his youth.

5. To prevent sexual sins: See what 1 Corinthians 7:2-5 says:

Nevertheless, to avoid fornication, let every man have his own wife, and let every woman have her own husband. [3]Let the husband render unto the wife due benevolence: and likewise also the wife unto the husband. [4]The wife hath not power of her own body, but the husband: and likewise also the husband hath not power of his own body, but the wife. ⁵Defraud ye not one the other, except it be with consent for a time, that ye may give yourselves to fasting and prayer; and come together again, that Satan tempt you not for your incontinency.

6. To fulfill the mandate of God to man in Genesis Chapter 1: 28 to be fruitful and replenish the earth.

    And God blessed them, and God said unto them, Be fruitful, and multiply, and replenish the earth, and subdue it: and have dominion over the fish of the sea, and over the fowl of the air, and over every living thing that moveth upon the earth.

Truth No 3: There is a BONE from you and of you SOMEWHERE.

But bones must come to their bones, and flesh must come to where they belong (Ezekiel37:7). How can they come together except they meet?

Mat 13: 24 – 30 explains this further:

…..Behold, a sower went forth to sow; [4]And when he sowed, some seeds fell by the way side, and the fowls came and devoured them up: [5]Some fell upon stony places, where they had not much earth: and forthwith they sprung up, because they had no deepness of earth: [6]And when the sun was up, they were scorched; and because they had no root, they withered away. [7]And some fell among thorns; and the thorns sprung up, and choked them: [8]But other fell into good ground, and brought forth fruit, some an hundredfold, some sixtyfold, some thirtyfold.

Your bone is somewhere waiting for you. Your life is like a seed. Where "you" fall matters in life and destiny. Our fulfillment in life is environmentally determined. You must fall on the right soil to get the right result – similarly, you must be in the right environment to find your bone.

Where is your life now? …On the way side, on the rock, among thorns or on the good soil? May you work with

God to get into your good land! Even within the good soil, productivity varies – 100 percent, 60 percent or 30 percent. This is what determines how much people enjoy their marriages.

You cannot marry unless you have LOCATED or have been LOCATED. Who said that none shall lack/want her mate? Is God a liar? God forbid: Yea, let God be true, but every man a liar…. (Roman 3:4). You may need to change your LOCATION to be LOCATED or to LOCATE thus REPOSITIONING.

Truth No 4: There is a KINGDOM key for MARRIAGE.

No marriage can take place without locating or being located. All marriages took place because somebody was found or found somebody. What am I saying?

Matthew 16:19:

"And I will give unto thee the KEYS of the kingdom of heaven: and whatsoever thou shalt bind on earth shall

be bound in heaven: and whatsoever thou shalt loose on earth shall be loosed in heaven."

God has given unto us the **keys** of the kingdoms – keys not key. There are different keys for different life issues. Prayer is not the primary key to locate or to be located! This is what I told the Leadership Certificate Course class in Dar es Salaam Tanzania in May 2010. God has given us the key of seed sowing for wealth and riches (Gen 8:22); the key of taking care of the poor for divine deliverances (Ps 41:1 – 3); the key of prayer and fasting for healing and divine health (James 5: 13 – 15), etc.

What key(s), therefore, did He give for locating and being located? Keys of looking, positioning (and re-positioning).

Let us take a walk through some Biblical examples:

1. **Adam and Eve** – Gen 2: 22-23

   And the rib, which the LORD God had taken from man, made he a woman, and brought her unto the man. ²³And Adam said, This is now

> **bone of my bones, and flesh of my flesh: she shall**
> **be called Woman, because she was taken out**
> **of Man.**

Note the woman was brought to the man, the man looked and recognized her as his bone and flesh and took her for a wife. God is still in the process of bringing men and women together, but only s/he that recognizes and agrees he has found/she has been found is established. God organized this book for some of you because your life partner could be right where you are now. Are your eyes open? Are you looking? For the sisters, are you properly positioning yourselves? Eve was at the right place at the right time in the right attitude and appearance; Adam's eyes were open at the right time, and he made the right decision for the right period.

Who said that a woman has no role to play? What if Eve refused to follow God to Adam? What if when Adam saw her, she was unkempt or arrogant? What

if she refused to accept Adam as bone of his bone?
Women have role; significant role to play.

2. **Isaac and Rebekah** – Gen 24:15 – 22:

And it came to pass, before he had done speaking,
that, behold, Rebekah came out, who was born
to Bethuel, son of Milcah, the wife of Nahor,
Abraham's brother, with her pitcher upon her
shoulder.

[16]And the damsel was very fair to look upon, a
virgin, neither had any man known her: and she
went down to the well, and filled her pitcher, and
came up. [17]And the servant ran to meet her, and
said, Let me, I pray thee, drink a little water of
thy pitcher.

[18]And she said, Drink, my lord: and she hasted,
and let down her pitcher upon her hand, and
gave him drink. [19]And when she had done giving

him drink, she said, I will draw water for thy camels also, until they have done drinking.

²⁰And she hasted, and emptied her pitcher into the trough, and ran again unto the well to draw water, and drew for all his camels. ²¹And the man wondering at her held his peace, to wit whether the LORD had made his journey prosperous or not.

²²And it came to pass, as the camels had done drinking, that the man took a golden earring of half a shekel weight, and two bracelets for her hands of ten shekels weight of gold;

Look at how the Bible described Rebekah in vs. 16 – Damsel was fair to look upon (excellent appearance, good dressing, good hair do, good body scent – not offensive, good makeup, good smile on her face, good in everything), a virgin, neither had any man known her (pure, innocent and fragile). Why did Abraham's eldest servant take notice of her?

a.   Promptness; Before he had done speaking, Rebekah came out...vs. 15; Rebekah went down to the well; Rebekah filled her pitcher, Rebekah came up (vs. 16). All this while the servant was watching.

b.   Hospitality, respect and good manners (vs. 18). Drink, my Lord, she said.

c.   Proper training (vs. 18). She was not sluggish and lackadaisical rather she hasted, and let down her pitcher upon her head, and gave him drink. She knew what and how to do, she knew how to treat strangers, she had a heart of gold.

d.   Sensitivity and compassion (vs. 19). I will draw water for your camels also, until they have done drinking. It takes an enormous amount of water to satisfy a camel but in this case, there were camels! Not "take and draw yourself, after all you are a man!" No!

Good appearance, manner, sensitivity and hospitality were counting for her. What is counting for you?

e.   Diligence (vs. 20). She hasted, emptied her pitcher…and ran again…and drew for all camels. What a worthy wife waiting just for the ideal man.

She did all this without knowing that somebody was watching. Do you know that there is a cloud of witnesses watching you daily and in places you least expect? This did not happen in church, office, or house. It happened in the field – may be in a bus stop, market place, concert, etc. people are watching and weighing.

In vs. 22 he decorated her before he knew who she was. God will decorate your life in this season. You want to marry?…emulate solved examples… many of you have deliberately or otherwise sent your God-given spouses far away by your behavior, dressing and attitude. But there is mercy in God right now.

    f.   What was Isaac's role? He did not just pray nor meditate? He did not just fast. He just lifted up his eyes and looked, and saw. Vs. 63.

> *And Isaac went out to meditate in the field at the eventide: and he lifted up his eyes, and saw, and, behold, the camels were coming. [64]And Rebekah lifted up her eyes, and when she saw Isaac, she lighted off the camel.*

    g.   What of Rebekah? Vs. 64. She too lifted up her eyes, saw and lighted from the camel. No pretending. She knew what she wanted. She asked questions, she went for it. Not saying 'it is the man's duty to find' or 'it is the man's duty to take the first steps'. She took a veil to cover herself…you cannot see everything at once. I am an onion. You will discover me; a little at a time.

But for some people, once a man says "I want to marry you" they move into his house – and become his cook, a bed mate, a "washer-woman", a cleaner, a messenger, a mother of his illegal children. No! Be an onion. Allow the man to discover you – one layer at a time.

She took a veil and covered herself.

h.   Isaac brought her home. He did the right things before claiming her. Vs. 67.

1.   **Jacob and Rachel:** Gen 28:6, 9, 17.

> *And he said unto them, Is he well? And they said, He is well: and, behold, Rachel his daughter cometh with the sheep.⁹And while he yet spake with them, Rachel*

came with her father's sheep; for she kept them. *¹⁷Leah was tender eyed; but Rachel was beautiful and well favoured.*

What made Rachel the preferred?

a. Recommendation by the public vs. 6 – Rachel, his daughter cometh with the sheep.

b. Consistency – **....behold, Rachel his daughter cometh with the sheep.** It was a daily routine that she was known for. Even the community could state with certainty when she would be appearing.

c. Diligence – vs. 9 – while he yet spake, she came. She was on time (on schedule) and at the right place. Jacob did not need to wait and be disappointed. She did not stay back home with excuses, but while he yet spake, she came. How positively predictable are you? Can people say something good about you? How dependable, reliable, and trustworthy are you? You must position yourself for victory in marriage.

d.   Beautiful and well favoured against tender eyed. Vs 16. Who will leave a beautiful, hardworking, well favoured woman for a tender eyed one? Why are others marrying and nobody is saying 'hello sister'? Are you tender eyed?

e.   What of Jacob? Vs 10 – 11: When he saw, he went near her, he rolled away the stone (relevance), he watered the flocks (diligence), he kissed Rachel (commitment), he lifted up his eyes and wept (emotional). Men are not the emotionless people the world is painting. Many women will always fall for a man whose emotions are real and evident.

Jacob was willing to serve for 14 years for her. How much are people willing to pay for your sake? How far can your friends go to get you? How precious are you to people around you? What will be missing when you are not around? Ask yourself, if I am to be a commodity in the market, how much will people be willing to pay for my head?

6. **Moses and Zipporah:** Ex 2: 16 – 17

> *Now the priest of Midian had seven daughters: and they came and drew water, and filled the troughs to water their father's flock.*
>
> *[17] And the shepherds came and drove them away: but Moses stood up and helped them, and watered their flock.*

Zipporah came to water her father's flock when she met Moses. Who told you they would find you at home – sitting, praying and fasting? Or while watching DSTV, GoTV or MyTV channels and all the soap operas in the local stations. It is only those that are well located (***positioned***) that are located (***found***)!

7. **Ruth and Boaz:** Ruth 3: 1 – 18:

And she went down unto the floor, and did according to all that her mother in law bade her. [7]And when Boaz had eaten and drunk, and his heart was merry, he went to lie down at the end of the heap of corn: and she came softly, and uncovered his feet, and laid her down.

[8]And it came to pass at midnight, that the man was afraid, and turned himself: and, behold, a woman lay at his feet. [9]And he said, Who art thou? And she answered, I am Ruth thine handmaid: spread therefore thy skirt over thine handmaid; for thou art a near kinsman.

[10]And he said, Blessed be thou of the LORD, my daughter: for thou hast shewed more kindness in

the latter end than at the beginning, inasmuch as thou followedst not young men, whether poor or rich.

[11]And now, my daughter, fear not; I will do to thee all that thou requirest: for all the city of my people doth know that thou art a virtuous woman.

Ruth was so diligent that even the owner of the farm noticed her. Was it deliberate? No. It was a way of life. She worked from sun up to sun down. When instructed by her mother in law, she washed herself of every smell, anointed her body with the best perfume and oil, put on a good garment, and went to the house of Boaz. And when asked, she was specific to what she wanted, *I am Ruth thine handmaid: spread therefore thy skirt over thine handmaid; for thou art a near kinsman.*

What can we see in Ruth that gave her a glorious second chance in life?

a.   **Obedience** (vs. 6). She simply obeyed her mother-in-law. Although her suggestion may (if poorly executed) bring her shame and further reproach, she obeyed her mother-in-law without as much as raising any questions. To fast forward Mary's advice to Jesus disciples in John 2: 15; *...whatever He tells you to do, do it,* she did what she was told to do by her mentor - Naomi.

b.   **Diligence** (Ruth 2:2-11). Ruth exemplified diligence. Although the farm land was not theirs, she was willing to go to work early in the morning and work till paid staffs had all left the farm. This extra ordinary commitment exposed her to Boaz who further favoured her leading to the workers dropping some fruits and harvests on her way. Her continued commitment made her the owner's favorite even before she met him.

c. **Beautification** (vs. 3): When it was time to go to Boaz on her mother-in-law's directives, she took her time to prepare herself. She took her birth, cleaned up herself, anointed herself and wore the best of her dresses before going to Boaz. This must have played a major role in attracting her to Boaz and thus she obtained favour from God and from Boaz.

d. **Positioning** (vs. 7): When she arrived at Boaz's house, without being told, she positioned herself at the foot of Boaz. Since in Biblical concept, we possess with our legs, she rightly positioned herself where she knew that Boaz cannot refuse her. Her positioning gave Boaz no option but to possess her.

e. **Wisdom** (vs. 9): When Boaz spoke to her, her responses were laced with wisdom. She was sure of what she wanted, was specific in her request and gave excellent reasons why she should be accepted. This made her a sought-after. Her attitude also exemplified wisdom. Thus, Boaz was willing to go the extra mile to have her even at a high cost and as early as possible.

f. **Right choice** (v10). She was not after "Mr. Perfect" or the young, but after the RIGHT. Despite the age difference, she was willing to do the right thing. In the next chapter, I will be discussing the age factor.

g. **Virtuous woman** (vs. 11): She was described by Boaz as a virtuous woman. Her shadow went ahead of her and made her a must take for Boaz.

What about Boaz? Despite having taken some drinks that night, Bible said that he saw, he was sensitive and then the very next day, he took steps.

What are you waiting for? Don't you know that the more you wait, the more you waste?

The story of Ruth also exemplifies the place of second chance. Our God is a God of second chance. He is willing to give you (a widow or widower reading this book) a second chance. Irrespective of how much you loved your spouse, the relationship ended at his/her death. Bible says, "Till death do you part." Death is a divinely permissible reason to remarry. Now that your spouse is dead, God is saying, if you are less than sixty years old, REMARRY. *Note that people above 60 years can also marry and remarry- and we have seen a number in our life time.* So, do not allow age to hinder you as marriage is God's provision for us here on earth to enjoy. In heaven, there is no marriage as we all are like angels. Therefore, do not MISS the opportunity to have the best of marriage as God ordained it.

Begin by properly positioning yourself for a new life. That is the desire of God. And I know that this is also the desire of your dead spouse. Free yourself from the past and move on the great future God has prepared for you. See you soon in your totally restored position.

To marry, therefore, our sisters must be well positioned. If currently poorly positioned, it is time for re-positioning. This is because until you re-position yourself, you have no position in life. In what areas are you expected to reposition? We shall be discussing this in the next chapter.

CHAPTER 4

Re-Positioning to be Located

Until you are rightfully positioned, you
cannot obtain your divine position

Every believer who desires to get married must be well positioned, just like the Biblical examples shown above in Chapter 3. You must be properly positioned to be positioned by God in marriage. Repositioning is needed by all – single sisters and brothers. Whether you are a spinster, bachelor, single parent, widow or widower, etc. repositioning is needed. In today's contemporary world, in what areas should you re-position yourself?

1. **Re-position in character:** *Live right.* To be located, you must be a woman/man of character. Your character defines who you are. Anyone who lacks character lacks value. Your charisma may attract people to you, but it takes your character to keep them with you. Do you know that many fallen Christians fell, not because Satan was strong, but because they lacked character? It takes just a slight crack in your character to fall from an all-time height in life to the mud.

    Billy Graham said **"If you lose your money, you have lost nothing; if you lose your health, you have lost something, but if you lose your character, you have lost everything."**

    Character is everything. Have this consciousness that someone (maybe your long-awaited life partner and God) is always watching. You cannot be sure who is watching per time, but you can be rest assured, you are constantly under divine and physical surveillance. God's eyes are over the whole earth watching, weighing and rewarding. He will mark you right in Jesus name.

Watch what you do whenever you think that nobody is watching. Watch what you do as you enter a taxi, a house, office, the church of God, as you serve in your units and departments, and as you negotiate with people. Someone, somewhere, all the time is watching.

2. **Re-position in words:** *Speak right.* Your words form and shape your world and destiny. God created the world we live in through His glorious words (Gen 1: 1 – 31, John 1: 1-3). He made you in His image so that you too can create your expected world with your words. The best word to speak is the scriptures.

    The tongue is a major weapon. It can result in stagnation or life advancement. Use it to your advantage. Do not use it against yourself. Until you speak it, the angel (or devil) will not pick it. Until they pick it, God (or Satan) will not perform it. That is why the Book of life says that life and death are in the power of the tongue (Proverb 18:21). Christ said that out of the abundance of the heart, the mouth speaks (Matt12:34). Until your mind is right, your mouth may never speak right.

More importantly, God is watching and people too. Do you know that many singles have lost their spouses by wrong use of words? When you are seen quarrelling over little things, do you know who is watching? When you are speaking like unbelievers and sharing dirty jokes as is commonly seen in our society today or on-line/Internets do you know who is watching? When you are seen shouting over nothing just because somebody provoked you, do you know who is watching? Your life partner may have been on his/her way to you only to see you demonstrating and decides to just turn back and ask God to speak again.

There are always better ways of telling somebody who proposed to you that your answer is no. Do not hurt people with your words. Do not spout out words with the excuse that is the way you feel; choose your words carefully, be polite. However, be assertive, let your stance be clear. And be sure not to lie. For instance; "I will pray about it/Let me hear from God"; "I am committed now"; "I am not considering that for now, unless the Lord tells me otherwise". A lot of time it is not so much of what is said but how it is said. Do not destroy the lives of people by your words. These are enemies of fruitful and blissful marital destiny. The Bible says in Job 6:25:

How forcible are right words! but what doth your arguing reprove? And in Proverbs, Solomon said: *A soft answer turneth away wrath: but grievous words stir up anger.* (Proverbs 15:1).

Remember, a man shall eat good by the fruits of his lips. May your lips procure only good to you for the rest of your life.

3. **Re-position in appearance:** *Look right.* "The way you **dress** determines the way you are ad**dress**ed" is a common saying within the Winners' family worldwide. How you look will to a large extent determine where you end. Looking good takes you ahead. People first see your looks before they hear your words.

How do you dress? Do you dress like a lady looking for a husband or like a girl looking for a "one-night stand"? Do you dress like a lady who a God-fearing man will be proud to present to his friends and family, or like a prostitute? When you dress wrongly, you may be telling men that you are available for short-term use but not for long-term marriage.

Also being a born-again Christian is not a reason to take your looks for granted. Destinies are grounded when issues of life like dressing are taken for granted. Carry yourself with dignity. Be decent and yet attractive. Can somebody proudly take you to the altar the way you are dressed right now to minister to God's people? If the answer is no, then you are wrongly dressed.

To the young men looking for a woman to marry; how is your appearance? Are you dressed like a responsible man or one of the touts in town, a displaced refugee or a beggar? Can a godly sister with Christian values be proud to walk along the street with you? Will her friends laugh at her for accepting and presenting you to them as her would-be husband?

You do not necessarily need expensive clothes. You only need to wear them (clothes) well. If shirts; please iron and tuck them in very well. If suits, make sure they do not smell. How often do you change your socks and under-wears? Are you among the low waist jeans boys? What value does your dressing present to the world?

Do you have body odour? Do you have mouth odour? If yes, address them. Your body odour may result from dirty and unwashed under-wears. How frequently do you wash your under-wears? Because they are not visible does not mean that they should be dirty. They announce themselves through the ugly scent that they emit. Is your hair well kept? How about your finger nails? I do not mean expensive make ups, but just look good. **Locating is 85 percent physical and 15 percent spiritual.** Are you presentable? Do you have a smile on your face always or a 'come not near' countenance? Your smile is the best complement to your dressing.

Adam looked, and what he saw he liked and thus he announced, "This is the bone of my bone and flesh of my flesh." Isaac looked and what he saw he liked, and he walked towards her. Jacob looked and fell in love with Rachel. You must look good if you desire to be found or to find the right child of God.

Destroy and clean up your mind from those beliefs that yours is yours and will come irrespective of how you look. That is not true. Many have lost their spouses to their better dressed-better looking roommates, classmates, friends and colleagues. Make up your mind to always look good. Remember God, angels and men/women are watching, weighing and rewarding.

May you never be so unlucky to have your spouse come on the day you dressed wrongly! So good dressing should not just be to the church, but at all times. Even as you jog in the morning, as you go to work or market. Make sure that at all times, you are very presentable. The key here is not how much, but how well!

4. **Re-position in activities.** *Keep yourself.* It is important that you understand that God has made

you a god so that you can take charge on earth (Ps82:6, Gen1:28). He gave you a brain so that He can rest while you gain. You are responsible for your life and must therefore keep yourself from destruction. You must keep yourself away from Satan and his agents. You must keep yourself away from temptations and trials. Acts 15:29 tells us to keep *'ourselves from fornication'* and other things.

John advises that as little children we should keep ourselves from idols (1 John 5:21). Jude tells us where to keep ourselves (Jude 1:21). You are still a spirit in a body. Anyone who exposes himself to issues of the flesh is set to fall.

What should you keep yourself from? From fornication, adultery, masturbation, homosexuality, lies and hypocrisy. Hebrews 13: 4 says that marriage is honorable when the bed is undefiled. Do not give the devil room to creep into your family. All sexual sins are against the temple of the Holy Ghost (your body).

Note that the foundation of your new home is built in courtship and if the foundation be destroyed, what can the righteous do? (Ps11:3). I often say that the big sins we see and hear of today began as small "insignificant" thoughts which matured and were tried out. The guide is do not start what you cannot (or do not want to) finish. Do not create an environment that fuels the situation. It all begins from the mind! Purge your heart. "It does not matter" often matters a lot. The people who fornicate may have started by saying, "it is fine as long as I would eventually marry him/her". Then, when they find that the marriage plans did not work; they are faced with a new mindset "This is not my first time, God probably understands that I cannot hold myself…" Before you know it, adultery become just another sin, then homosexuality and all forms of mental deprivation as we find in the world today (also elaborated on in Romans 1:26-32).

It usually begins small. Neap it at the bud, do not let it mature. And even if you believe you are already neck deep into sin; hear this, it does not matter how far you have gone on a wrong route; as soon as you discover your error make a turnaround journey. Note what the scriptures says in Ps85:8

> *I will hear what God the LORD will speak: for he will speak peace unto his people, and to his saints: BUT LET THEM NOT TURN AGAIN TO FOLLY.*

Today is your day for a total turnaround. Turn now. Again, I say, TURN!

Also, while in service in God's house, keep yourself. While sweeping as a sanctuary keeper, while protecting vehicles as a security officer, while guiding people to their seats as an usher, while singing in the choir, while testifying at the altar, while teaching children in the Sunday school, while instructing first timers and new converts as hospitality member, while evangelizing, counseling and praying for those in need, keep yourself.

People locate and are located while they do their normal daily activities. Have you ever wondered while doctors marry a lot of nurses, teachers marry themselves (like my parents), bankers marry bankers, etc.? People are seen in the place of their day to day activities.

The next person you are guiding to his seat maybe your God ordained husband/wife, the person seating by you in a church service maybe your spouse, the fellow working with you while you clean the toilet as a sanctuary keeper maybe the appointed individual for you. Even the pastor or deacon receiving your testimony maybe the ordained person for you! Keep yourself. Be always mindful that God and people are watching. You are never sure when and where you will meet the person, thus portray the picture of the true you.

I found my wife on phone. I know of a couple that found themselves on Facebook. My sister in-law met her husband through recommendations. I know a couple that found themselves in Sunday school, another during prison evangelism, etc. The methods and places vary. Therefore, keep yourself. My wife (even though so beautiful and wonderful) may have lost me if her countenance and response on the phone on June 23rd, 1999 was unfavourable or non-hospitable. Since you are not sure what route God will be sending the person through, like the boys scout, **be prepared always**. Live ready.

5. **Re-position in the market.** *Touch right.* This is not a topic many people will like to hear, but led by the Spirit, I will talk about it. Many believers are victims of this – touching what they should not

or allowing people touch them where they should not! The world is a marketplace – people are always pricing, assessing, and buying one thing or the other.

The conventional marketplace is one place that most believers let go on regular basis. Several behave as if they are in the market. Some steal, some fight, some cheat, and others dress anyhow. But whether in the open market, supermarkets, or anywhere out there, your behavior is important. Therefore, touch right.

If somebody takes you to the market (whether in courtship or as a friend), behave yourself. Avoid covetousness (I Tim 6:6). It could be a trial. Someone will say, but 'I have to be myself sometimes'. Yes. Be yourself always, not just sometimes – but make sure it is what God said you should be. Be careful what shops you enter and what you allow the traders do to you. I have seen sisters and brothers misbehaving in markets in the name of bargaining. When a sister desires to buy on credit, she may even allow an unbeliever touch her unnecessarily. This is evil.

What you cannot afford, you do not need. Stop buying food, jewelries and clothes on credits. Stop taking loans to change wardrobes, buy cars or even to buy food. This has made a number of good Christians lose their salvation. Debt is an avoidable burden. People say that window shopping is free. Yes. But it could also lead to other avoidable sins. Stop window shopping, it may lead to covetousness. Watch what you always do, especially in the market.

The market place can also be reckoned with in locating a life partner. I once heard of a lady who was nicknamed "tasting". Why? Because every man who proposed to her had an opportunity to have a taste of married life with her; the bed, the foods, the car rides etc. My sisters, do not make yourselves commodities in the market that can be bought on credit or even used before payment. Jesus Christ paid a high price for your redemption (and body)! Know your true worth. That a potential "customer" is bargaining or has made a part payment does not give him access or right of ownership to a priceless commodity as you!

As a brother, are you in the business of "pick and drop"? Do you have the target of going into courtship with all the sisters in church before you decide who to marry? How many sisters' hopes have you aroused and unduly dashed for selfish reasons? Remember that life is a seed and you reap the products of your seed! The next time you want to go into a relationship settle it within yourself and with God.

Be sure that when you set out to find faults; then you will certainly find them, abundantly too. After all, you will marry a human being not an angel. And do **you** honestly have no faults?!

6. **Re-position in attitude**: *Act right.* Have an attitude of gratitude. After my traditional marriage, we fixed our church wedding. It was just two months ahead. When I got my February salary, I sent over 90 percent of it to my wife to begin her preparations. This I did so excitedly knowing that somehow, I would survive. I was to use some left-over funds from the previous months to complete my tithe.

    Upon receiving the money, she replied and said, "…but it is not enough." I was so hurt that all through that weekend I was asking God questions – is she the one? Does she not know how much I make? Couldn't she even ask how would I survive the month? I was truly restless. By Sunday evening, I agreed with God that during our next call, if the first thing she says is not "Thank you", the marriage was over. Thank God, when I called her on Monday, she started by appreciating the gift. This was the pre-GSM era!

While going through this season of doubt, God asked me a question, "See how agitated you are over a small amount of money. How much have you thanked me for all I have done for you – life, air, food, mental soundness, sleep, shelter, security, etc.? This encounter changed my whole worship and life style. Then I understood what He meant when He said, *"In everything give thanks: for this is the will of God in Christ Jesus concerning you."* (I Thessalonians5:18). And again, Paul said in Philippians 4:6: *Be careful for nothing; but in everything by prayer and supplication with thanksgiving let your requests be made known unto God.*

God appreciates people who are grateful in small or big things; and so do men. When somebody gives you a lift, thank him/her; when a door is opened for you, say thanks; and when you are shown care; be grateful. When somebody of his/her own accord sends you a gift, GSM credit, (no matter the value), appreciate the person. Build the attitude of gratitude into your life. An act of gratitude procures several additional favors.

Other relevant attitudes are those of "**can do**" and "**does do**". No one loves a lazy person. Work to be relevant in other peoples' lives. Work to help in things you know how to do. Do not wait to be asked, volunteer to help. Life is a product of the contributions we make. Be an addition into someone's life and you will never lack good friends. Do not procrastinate and put off for tomorrow what you can conveniently do today. Be proactive in words and action.

Remember important dates and appreciate your friend(s) on such dates. Proverbs 18:24 says;

A man that hath friends must shew himself friendly: and there is a friend that sticketh closer than a brother.

Be a true friend. Show yourself as a friend. Work to make a difference in people's lives.

7. **Re-position in relationships:** *Walk right.* What kind of people are your friends? Who do you walk with? The Psalmist says:

    Blessed is the man that walketh not in the counsel of the ungodly, nor standeth in the way of sinners, nor sitteth in the seat of the scornful. (Psalm 1:1).

    Watch the relationships you keep and nourish. Whoever that is not adding to your life would be subtracting and therefore such a one should be subtracted. As long as your hands are full with relationships that are taking you nowhere, you may never have those that God has programmed for you. Many of us are walking now with the wrong people when the right ones are just by the corner waiting.

    The ring you are wearing as a spinster, who gave it to you? It could be one of the things that is turning people off from you. Where are you commonly seen – in the camp of divorcees/separated people or believers who are believing God with you or mentors? Be not deceived, evil communication corrupts good manners.

There are current ongoing relationships you may need to terminate if what you want is a marital bliss. There are phone numbers in your handset you may need to delete. There are calls you may need to make now to end some relationships. There are people you may need to subtract from your life. Remember, Proverb 13:20 reminds us that,

He that walketh with wise men shall be wise: but a companion of fools shall be destroyed.

8. **Re-position at home:** You must have a Christian home: A Christian home is not just a house where all are Christians or go to church on Sunday, but a Christ like home. A home administered with the principles of Jesus which represent God's ways and

styles. The authority of a believer is weakened by a home full of turmoil! Accept scriptural responsibility over the welfare of your home. Maintain financial and material integrity at home.

Can you cook? Can you maintain a clean house? What do people see when they visit? Dirty wears and wares everywhere, unwashed utensils, cobwebs and unhandled waste? When last did you clean your refrigerator and other electronics? Keep your home and surroundings clean. Your spouse maybe your next door neighbour!

Be hospitable to friends and strangers (Heb 13:1-2). By this many have entertained angels and their spouses unaware.

How do you handle visitors in your home? Do you know that your spouse can come to your doors unannounced and it is your attitude and reception that will determine whether he/she will come in, stay or go? Abraham's servant, Jacob and Moses were all unannounced when they found their wives. You will not miss your opportunity.

9. **Re-position in office:** *Work right.* You spend a large proportion of your time in the office. You meet staff, colleagues, customers and friends of the company/ organization on daily basis. Work right.

Show commitment to your work. Show diligence. Let integrity speak for you. Do not come to work by 8.00 am and write 7.30 am. Do not join others to slander fellow staff. Divorce yourself from the organization's gossip team. Come to work and do the work – that is why you are being paid. If you can, make sure that your job description is being exceeded. The Bible asks us to go an extra mile for anyone that asks us to go a mile.

By your work, set yourself at a higher level of performance. You have the Spirit of God, the mind of Christ and the wisdom of the ancient. You cannot but lead the group. God has promised to distinguish

you, and make you a Daniel of your age and time –
10 times better than your peers. Work to show the
world that God is superior.

10. **Re-position in church**: *Serve right*. Why is it
that most Christian marriages in the church
involve kingdom stewards? Divine rewards! But in
addition – right positioning. If a first timer comes,
who do you think he or she will see first – the usher
and then the chorister? He may see the technical
unit as they move around with their instrument
or operate the camera, the security and traffic as
they park their car, enter the bus or ensure proper
traffic control; the counselors and hospitality as they
welcome the first timers; or the evangelist as they
follow them up. But are these the only people in the
church? No. Kingdom services position you to be
found and to find. Finding and being found is one
of the additions mentioned in Mathew 6:33:

But seek ye first the kingdom of God, and his righteousness; and all these things shall be added unto you.

Is getting married the reason for serving God? No. But it is the desire of God for you to get married and He will break every protocol to satisfy your longing soul. The word even said the husband man that laboureth shall be the first partaker – including in marriage.

Again, where you are serving maybe where your second half is. The seat the usher directs you to maybe just next to him/her that will make a great difference in your life. Learn to obey simple instructions in the kingdom. Allow God to divinely perfect all that concerns you. Instead of making noise and claiming right, allow the Spirit of God to lead you to where the pastures are green and to where He has prepared for you.

Only God knows exactly where He has kept your blessings.

Let me end this chapter by speaking expressly to the men: What must brothers do to get married early and on time? What must they do to find the right sister as wives?

a. **Begin to look:** Lift up your eyes and look. Until you look and re-look, you may never find. Looking will require both physical and spiritual eyes. Engage them today. If you have been looking without finding, maybe you are looking in the wrong direction. Change your focus. Maybe you are not looking with the right intention or in the right direction. Maybe you are looking with your eyes fully or partly closed. It is wrong to do the same thing in the same way repeatedly and expect different results. Change your methods.

b. **Begin to take steps:** Stop waiting or you will waste. Start taking steps. Say something and do something. Great destinies are built on steps taken. Until you take steps, nothing good will happen. I know of a brother in church who feared telling a sister his intentions. He was advancing in age and had not been able to tell any sister that he wanted to marry her. He serves in the children's department. Over a period he met a sister in the same department and was convinced that she was his wife. But he found it difficult to take steps. Having prayed and prayed, one day he got enough strength and courage to take the needed steps. Then the miracle happened. As he approached the sister, the entire speech that he had prepared just disappeared. He was tongue tied. While standing there looking at the sister, the sister helped him out, "do not worry. I know what you want to say. You want to marry me. I agree." Short and simple. When last I heard of them, they had two children; a boy and a girl to the glory of God. How he wished he took those steps months earlier. Take steps. Only step takers can win in life. Are you afraid she will say no? Why not hope she will say yes? Both have a fifty-fifty probability (chance) of occurrence. Take that step now. Be ten times bold. Take steps.

c. **Be diligent**: Only the man with a diligent hand can sit with kings. After Moses took care of the cattle of Jethro, Jethro sent for him and made him his son-in-law as well as the keeper of the cattle. He that does not work, Bible said, should not eat. How can you marry if you cannot feed your wife (and later your children)? You need a home of your own. You need your own household goods. Your wife can only support your vision. Where are you headed? You must define yourself by your work. Work hard, work smart and work well.

Do you know that after salvation, the next most important life identifier is work? I am saved, Yes, and what next – What do you do? You are either identified as a Christian or by the work you do – a teacher, doctor, carpenter, farmer, etc. What are you known for? What is your occupation? Find one; if you cannot find one, create one. But, do something.

d. **Be compassionate:** Be ready to help, willing to communicate and ready to distribute; and by so doing, many have helped themselves into their marital destinies. Remember the story of Rebecca, Rachael, Jacob, Moses, etc. Be compassionate. Be willing to help others in need. Be ready to distribute what you have and share. Care for others and learn to be good to both people we know and those we do not know. Be kind.

Basic qualification of an IDEAL Christian life partner

1. **Fear of God.** Marry a man or woman that fears and loves God and not somebody that just loves you. You need God to make your marriage work. But God can only come in if invited by a couple that fears and loves Him. A continuous love for God is a guaranteed backbone for a sweet and enjoyable marital destiny. One of the things that convinced

me that my wife was the right person was her love for God at that time. By then, I was not an ordained worker, but I knew where I was going and having a woman who was completely sold out to God was a needed and basic requirement. It will make my life easier. So, I went all out for her.

Do not court an unbeliever. It is disastrous. Bible speaks against being unequally yoked with unbelievers. Also, do not date married men/women. You will be sinning against God as well as sowing dangerous seeds against your own marital and generational destiny. There is no justification for either going out with a Muslim or a married man. Both are destiny destroyers.

2. **Respect women/men:** A man or woman that normally respects the opposite sex is more likely to respect you when you marry. But somebody that easily talks down on people will also easily talk down on you at the least provocation.

3. **Honour parents:** Marry a man/woman that honours his/her own parents (and your parents as well). This is a divine commandment. More so, life is a seed. Be sure to sow the kind of seed you will enjoy its fruits. If s/he does not have regards for his/her parents; soon it will be your parents' turn and then yours. This is vital for a viable management of in-laws.

4. **Have compassion for other people:** A man/woman that normally has compassion for others, who is moved by other people's challenges will at the hour of need be moved by your challenges and issues. Selfishness is not the nature of Christ or He would not have torn the wall of partition and invited everyone to enjoy kingdom beauty and splendor.

5. **Have an attitude of gratitude:** One who appreciates simple things from God and people will not take you for granted. Gratitude oils every relationship. It is, therefore, important that the fellow appreciates

simple things as well as big things. Observe her/his attitude when gifts are given. I tell you, anybody that does not appreciate small things, will soon not appreciate big things. Learn from those who have gone ahead of you – look out for somebody that has an attitude of gratitude always.

6. **Is diligent and hardworking:** Every house is built by some man, but the builder of all things is God. It takes diligence and hard work to build. It is actually easier to destroy and bring down, than to build. Only the diligent will sit with kings and great men. It takes diligence to make money to run the home, it takes diligence to keep the house clean and tidy, it takes diligence to cook when you are dead tired from the day's work, it takes diligence to bathe the children when what you really want to do is sleep and or rest. Diligence before marriage is needed to have diligence after marriage. I remember when I was told that my wife was a hard worker and a home maker; I was excited because that means

I have found the right person. How do people describe you?

7. **Have a vision.** Women are given to men as wives to be help meets – helps in running their life vision. If the man has no vision, then there will be nothing to run and this is a major crisis in most homes. When the man has no vision, the woman becomes the visioner and this is against the covenant and usually leads to family crisis. I am not saying that women should not have visions, but that their visions should support their husbands' vision. Now when a man has no vision, what will the woman's vision support? It ends up standing alone and this may be a challenge to a godly home.

The Age Factor:

You will discover that from all my discussion, I have not mentioned age as a factor. Why? Because it is not a significant factor in the Bible if the person is physically old enough to be called a man or woman! Or let me say, it is not as significant as people make it. We were told that Abraham was about 10 years older than Sarah. But that was where it ended. Nobody ever mentioned age again between couples – Adam and Eve, Adam was created before Eve. But what of Isaac and Rebekah, Jacob and Rachel, Joseph and Mary, Zachariah and Elizabeth, etc. Age was never a factor in their marriages. Nowhere did we see anybody asking how old a woman is before proposing!

I also saw Boaz commending Ruth for not making age a priority in her choice of a second husband.

"The LORD bless you, my daughter," he replied. "This kindness is greater than that which you showed earlier: You have not run after the younger men, whether rich or poor." (Ruth 3:10).

Is age completely irrelevant? No. But it should not be the primary determining factor in marriage. I have seen men that married women who are older than them and they still had excellent relationship (and vice versa). I have also seen women that married older men and had good marriages. In some part of Nigeria, a good number of same age marriages have good marital lives. What we need to ask ourselves is, "Am I proud of this person? Can I live with this person? Are there irreconcilable differences that I cannot live with?"

The point is this: happiness in marriage is not age or qualifications determined. Find out what God is saying about the situation; He is your father.

CHAPTER 5

ENEMIES OF MARITAL BLISS

What you have not handed over to God, remains unhandled.

When you have FOUND (or have been FOUND), remember that the journey has not ended, but, it is the real beginning of a true and life transforming journey. There will be the period of courtship during which you get to know yourselves, reveal personal (sometimes very private) secrets, share beliefs and visions. In addition, this is the season when great decisions are made pertaining where to live, where to worship, what vision(s) to pursue, how many children to have, what kind(s) of friends to keep, and very importantly, how to manage your family finances.

This is the period when high level sensitivity in the spirit is mandatory. That you have 'found' or 'is found' does not end your work for a fulfilling marital destiny. It ends the physical search and marks the beginning of the spiritual confirmation or approval.

Now it is important to recognize that according to 1Cor 16:9: *…a great door and effectual is opened unto you, and there are many adversaries*. Marital bliss is a great door that is opened, but there are many anti-happiness adversaries. It is now time to contend in prayer (Deuteronomy 2:24).

Now that God has given you your life partner, it is spiritual battle time. Several issues will arise that will make you want to change your mind. Some maybe appearances of the devil! If you are not sensitive, you may make a wrong decision – like my anger at my wife over not saying thanks when I gave her my salary. You must be ready to fight the good fight of faith.

Spiritual Courtship

Courtship period is a period of discoveries – the good, the bad, and sometimes, the ugly. Things are not always what they look like at first glance. If you discover some things that you cannot live with nor resolve, please feel very free to end the relationship and return to stage 1: **searching.** Broken courtship is a blessing, but divorce is a curse.

It is, however, the time to PRAY. Pray and Fast. To establish your tomorrow in God, you MUST make God your marital senior partner as early as possible. After finding my wife, although we were in different cities at that time, we began early morning prayers (5 am every day). This has continued till today. In addition, we also began Wednesday fasting and prayers. This was the time when Living Faith Church (our local assembly) had twice mid-week program on Tuesdays and Thursdays. We fasted and prayed for our marriage and future together. It among other things brought us closer. On some of the days (when we could afford it), we prayed on phone together to break the fast.

It is, therefore, very crucial at this stage for you to commit your life and relationship to God.

Hear the Psalmist in Psalm 37:5

Commit thy way unto the LORD; trust also in him; and he shall bring it to pass.

Allow God into your relationship and He will perfect it.

Major enemies of marital bliss:

What are the common enemies you must fight at this time?

1. **Past experiences:** Especially in relationship: You may have had some very bad experiences in life. Forget them. All men/women are not like the previous partners. You may have gotten into several messes and disappointments because you chose to trust someone, choose to trust again. The Bible says in Romans 8: 28-32:

And we know that all things work together for good to them that love God, to them who are the called according to his purpose. ²⁹For whom he did foreknow, he also did predestinate to be conformed to the image of his Son, that he might be the firstborn among many brethren. ³⁰Moreover whom he did predestinate, them he also called: and whom he called, them he also justified: and whom he justified, them he also glorified. ³¹What shall we then say to these things? If God be for us, who can be against us? ³²He that spared not his own Son, but delivered him up for us all, how shall he not with him also freely give us all things?

Hear what the scripture said: all things work together for good…not that all things are good. They may not look good right now, but they work together for your good. The disappointments also work together for your good so long as you are

111

among *them that love God*. For if God be for you, who can be against you?

Therefore, forget the past and move on with the future. The past is in the grave – you cannot do anything about it; the present is here – it is your only currency; and the future is in the womb – determined by what you do with today the present. Like Paul in Philippians 3:13: ***forgetting those things which are behind, and reaching forth unto those things which are before, ¹⁴ I press toward the mark for the prize of the high calling of God in Christ Jesus.***

Forget the past. Reach out to the future. Have you been disappointed, put the past away. Go for the prize of His high calling –in this case, marriage. Remember not the former things. God is about to do something new (Is 43:18 – 19).

2. **Parental lifestyle and relationship:** Several singles come from families where marriages were

warfare. They saw their parents fight and quarrel so frequently with sometimes, various levels of physical abuse. Mothers (and sometimes, fathers) were beaten, battered and reproached right before their children. Maybe it was not your parents who had marital problems, but your uncles, sisters, aunty, or other relations. Based on this, some singles have come to believe that marriage is not good. This is a lie of the devil.

My parents had an excellent relationship by all standards. I never saw my father and mother quarrel openly all through the life time of my father. I desired to have what they had. And today I can boldly say I have more. But I could not say the same for all my siblings. On one occasion, I cried as I treated one of my sisters after yet another fight with her husband, her body was full of injuries. It was so bad that I had to give her strong pain relievers before she could sleep.

You too may have seen the good, the bad, and the ugly in one or more marriages. However, the truth is that marriage is GOOD. I have several believers whose marriages are enviable. Some waited on God for the fruit of the womb for over a decade post marriage, but still had enviable homes. Yes, today God has blessed them with children – but even in the absence of children, they have good lives.

You can decide today to have a good home. Good and enjoyable marriage is a choice and not a gift. You can make a choice to rewrite the history of your family with an excellent marriage. If marriage was not good, God would have told us; unless you are saying that God lied. But we all know that it is impossible for God to lie.

3. **Bitterness and hatred:** In life, offences must come. But the Bible says: Woe to him by whom they come. It is time to let go. Previous offences, strives and hatred for past disappointments draw us back.

Bitterness and hatred hardly hurt the person hated, but the person carrying it.

Hear what Hebrew 12:15 says:

Looking diligently lest any man fail of the grace of God; lest any root of bitterness springing up trouble you, and thereby many be defiled;

It is you that is troubled and defied not the person you hate. It is the person who is carrying bitterness that will fail. My Bishop would say, "you can never be bitter and be better" Run from bitterness. It has never helped anybody. Let go, and let God take over.

4. **Culture and traditions:** We come from a culture where we believe that it must be the man that will take the first step. That is ok. But, as a lady, you must also make yourself accessible so that he can find you. Make his work easier by re-positioning

yourself to be found and located. Stop hiding behind the doors.

We also come from a culture that believes that age and career paths are vital in making marital decisions. This is not always the case. Allow God to guide and direct you. Marriage is a spiritual exercise. Do not "carnalize" it.

5. **Doubts:** Doubts are enemies of divine intervention. When we live in doubts, we deny ourselves of divine visitations. When we are suspicious of everything, we miss the mark of His high calling. God looks at the heart before He blesses.

Like wisdom, good marriages are from God. And as I said earlier, you must contend for it in prayers. But see what He is saying from James 1:6-8

If any of you lack wisdom, let him ask of God, that giveth to all men liberally, and upbraideth not; and it shall be given him. ⁶But let him ask in

faith, nothing wavering. For he that wavereth is like a wave of the sea driven with the wind and tossed. ⁷For let not that man think that he shall receive any thing of the Lord. ⁸A double minded man is unstable in all his ways.

If you are double minded in asking, God is not committed to give you.

6. **Sin:** Sin makes destinies to stink and to sink. You are not married until God has joined you in marriage. Living in sin denies you of supernatural support. Live-in-lovers are very common in some countries. That it is cultural or common does not make it right. No wonder you have so many frustrated young girls roaming the streets with children that have no identifiable fathers.

When you plan your marriage outside God, you are digging an early grave. I remember a sister in one of our churches that got married to a 'prophet'. She was warned against it by the counseling pastors. But since she believed she knew better than the pastors, she went on and married the man. Less than three months later, she was found dead, killed by the same man she professed that loved her. He killed her and left her in the house to decay. That shall not be your portion. Listen to your pastors, your spiritual mentors, and God. It is never too late to make the right decision.

Sin makes one lose the grace of God. Sin here goes far beyond adultery and fornication. Disobedience to parents (both spiritual and physical), lies, etc. are as dangerous. Therefore, adhere to the advice from Paul in Romans 6:13: ***Neither yield ye your members as instruments of unrighteousness unto sin: but yield yourselves unto God, as those that are alive from the dead, and your members as instruments of righteousness unto God.***

Some hate what they do, but cannot stop. It may be important to seek the counsel of God's servants for advice and prayers.

1. **Fear:** Fear destroys. It is an enemy of faith. Since without faith you cannot please God, living in fear makes you plan without God. You need to deal with the spirit of fear. A wise man defined fear as 'false evidences appearing real.' It has the capacity to demobilize your destiny. It makes a man unable to take the needed steps. It prevents a sister from properly positioning herself for kingdom victory. Fear keeps you imprisoned.

   The consequences of fear are as grave as unbelief: Revelation 21:8

   But the FEARFUL, and unbelieving, and the abominable, and murderers, and whoremongers, and sorcerers, and idolaters, and all liars, shall have their part in the lake which burneth with fire and brimstone: which is the second death.

Because of the devastating effects of fear, God in the above scripture classified it with murderers and idolaters. Consciously deal with fear. You have escaped already in Jesus name.

2. **Curses**: One other enemy of marital bliss is curses. This may be self-induced, family related, or could even be curses of men, devil/witches or of God/Law. This is again where contending for the faith becomes very important. Some have all manner of wickedness standing against their marital destinies. Some have forces covering them with veils making them inaccessible. Some have negative demonic odours following them. I have heard of beautiful ladies that have evil flies following them everywhere. And some have experienced the near miss syndrome so many times that they have almost given up. Anytime something good is just about to happen, something negative occurs; when they think they have found him/her – a problem emerges and scatters the whole relationship; when they have

saved enough money to take a good and positive step, some family crisis comes up and devours it all.

But Christ has redeemed us from the curse of the law (Galatians 3:13 – 14). It is therefore time for us to fight the good fight of faith. It is time to seek counsel from real men of God or Pastor. It is time to take a spiritual approach to solving the problems. Why? The things that are seen are formed from things unseen.

Please recognize that only the curse of God/Law is destroyed by redemption. After redemption, you must consciously work with God and His word to overcome the other four kinds of curses – self inflicted like curse of the thief; family like generational curses; man induced like parental curses (seen in Reuben) and witches and wizards like Balak and Balaam.

Recognize the problem, seek guidance and obey divine instructions. God will bring you completely out of it in Jesus name.

CHAPTER 6

GOD CAN AND WILL DO IT

It does not take time, it only takes God. God
is a specialist of sudden occurrences

There are things you must understand about God. These
include:

1. **God takes pleasure in your prosperity** – including
    your marital prosperity. He is fully interested in
    your well-being. Psalm 35:27

    Let them shout for joy, and be glad, that favour
    my righteous cause: yea, let them say continually,
    Let the LORD be magnified, which hath pleasure
    in the prosperity of his servant.

2. **God has a program and a plan to bless you.** These plans were there long before you were conceived in your mother's womb. Jeremiah 29:11

    For I know the <u>thoughts</u> that I think toward you, saith the LORD, thoughts of peace, and not of evil, to give you an expected end (KJV).

    For I know the <u>plans</u> I have for you, declares the LORD, plans for welfare and not for evil, to give you a future and a hope (English Standard Version).

    For I have known the thoughts that I am thinking towards you -- an affirmation of Jehovah; thoughts of peace, and not of evil, to give to you posterity and hope (Young Literal Translation).

3. **God has all it takes to bless you.** He made the entire world in six days. He has for eternity sustained the world by His word. He still controls the earth,

and all the silver and gold on earth are His including the cattle upon a thousand hills. Psalm 24:1

The earth is the LORD's, and the fulness thereof; the world, and they that dwell therein.

Also, the cattle upon a thousand hills are his (Psalm 50:10) and all the silver and gold in the world (Haggai 2:8)

4. **In Him is the fountain of life.** God has an unending supply of blessings including marital blessings. He is a caring, sharing and giving God and is willing to start new fountains as believers request for them. He also is very willing to impact light and advancement on as many as are willing to believe and receive. Psalm 36:9.

For with thee is the fountain of life: in thy light shall we see light.

Marital fountain is in Him. Accessing Him is accessing the good and great things He has in stock.

5. **God is more than able**. He gave Eve to Adam, Rebecca to Isaac, and Racheal to Jacob. He also gave wives to Joseph and Boaz. He gave husband to Rachael, Naomi and even a harlot called Rahab. He gave children to barren women – Sarah, Hannah, Elizabeth etc. He restored the home of David. God is able and more than able. Ephesians 3:20

Now unto him that is able to do exceeding abundantly above all that we ask or think, according to the power that worketh in us,

Also 1 Corinthians 2: 9 says: *But as it is written, Eye hath not seen, nor ear heard, neither have entered into the heart of man, the things which God hath prepared for them that love him.*

He is all you need to have a very fulfilling and exhilarating marital destiny. Outside Him you have nothing, but in Him, you have everything.

6. **God does not need any support from anyone.** He single-handedly made the earth and single-handedly sustains the earth. He single-handedly formed you in the womb, preserved you to delivery and has kept you till now. He single-handedly can bless you and keep you blessed. He can set you up in your marital destiny and establish your path. You do not need an alternative! Jeremiah 32:17, 27

Ah Lord GOD! behold, thou hast made the heaven and the earth by thy great power and stretched out arm, and there is nothing too hard for thee:...Behold, I am the LORD, the God of all flesh: is there anything too hard for me?

For with Him all things are possible. Is there anything too difficult for our God? Your marital destiny cannot be too hard for our God.

7. **He knows the bone of your bone and the flesh of your flesh**. He made you and blessed you. He decided without your consent who your parents will

be, where you will be born, which tribe and nation you will belong to, and what your martial destiny will be. He therefore before He formed thee, knew who the bone of your bone is and where he/she could be found. Your search outside of Him will only lead to frustration. Proverb 16: 25

There is a way that seemeth right unto a man, but the end thereof are the ways of death.

…the more you walk with Him, the easier it is to identify truly your bone and flesh, irrespective of where they are on planet earth.

8. **He is willing to walk with you to get you to your place of destiny**. He walked with Abraham and gave him a child at 100 years. Enoch walked with Him and was translated. Jesus walked with Him and came back to life. He desires to walk with you to take you to your bone and flesh. 3 John 2.

Beloved, I wish above all things that thou mayest prosper and be in health, even as thy soul prospereth.

9. **Only the diligent can make it to the place of destiny.** Slothfulness is anti-covenant. Procrastination is a key enemy of diligence. Proverbs 22:29

Seest thou a man diligent in his business? He shall stand before kings; he shall not stand before mean men.

God expects you to show you are serious. Are you determined and you are ready to be a wife/husband and a father/mother? It is time to show God that you are ready.

What then must you do to? Let me take you through the 9 Rs of Locating and be Located.

CHAPTER 7

9 Rs of Locating and Being Located

Re-Dream – You have dreamed before, but like Joseph, dream again. Do not just dream, document your dreams, share your dreams, and speak your dreams. What kind of spouse do you want? If you see one, will you recognize her/him? What are the qualities you are looking for in a potential spouse? Are they clear and precise or ambiguous and amorphous? Re-dream and share. Post your dreams on your mirror, table and everywhere your eyes go. Dreams are power and God respects our dreams.

Re-design your strategies – It is foolishness to keep doing the same thing the same way and expect a new or different result. Re-design your strategies. Learn from what you did that did not work, and change it to what may work. Learn from steps that failed and build a better strategy. Learn from activities of the past, and create a new part. Re-design your strategies and build on strategies that have worked or will work.

Re-activate your passion – Nobody will love to do anything with a passionless person. Passion is the springboard of life, the power behind love and the oil of lasting relationships. A passionless person will not succeed in anything – including marriage. Therefore, re-activate your passion. Yes, people may have failed you, you may have lost things, and somebody may have exploited your passion for things and even insulted you, but re-activate your passion. Get passionate. Be passionate. Ensure full passion in everything you do. Passion engenders friendships.

Re-ignite your zeal – Zeal drives, zeal overcomes obstacles, and zeal makes the impossible cheaply possible. Re-ignite your zeal. Like Joab, Jesus, etc., let people see your zeal for

God, for life, and for your career. Let people use you as an example of a zealous person. Let your zeal cause people to want to partner with you or marry you. Be zealous for something good – God, man, career, community welfare, etc.

Re-engineer your vision – Where there is no vision, the people perish. Your spouse is coming to support your vision. So, where there is no vision, no spouse is needed. Re-engineer your vision. If small, enlarge it. Remember you have a big God. So, allow God to help you expand and document your vision in a most challenging way. Amplify your vision, expand it, document it, share it and be proud of it. Tell everyone that needs to know what your vision is.

Re-work your plans – Do you have plans that have not worked over the years, re-work them. If you have no plans at all, develop one. You need plans to make your dream come to pass. Your plans should define and document what you have to do, when you have to do them, where you have to do them, with whom you have to do them, and at what cost you have to do them.

Your plans should answer the simple questions – **Why, what, when, where, who, how and how much**. For instance -Why do you want to marry? What do you want to do to get married? When do you want to marry? Who qualifies to be your spouse? Who can you plan with? How do you want to go about finding your spouse and executing the marriage process? How much are you planning on spending at the courtship, pre-marital and marital projects? Etc. Rework your plans to accommodate the recent changes in the environment - internet, GSM, Uber, etc. Do not tell me 'but I have a plan.' Did it work? If it did not work, re-plan.

Reposition yourself in the 10 dimensions - Looking at this book, you have to reposition yourself in character, words, appearance, activities, in the market, attitudes, relationship, home, office and work. You may need to reposition in all 10 departments or focus on the most critical one for you. By all means, reposition.

Release yourself and Relax on God– The Bible said, "having done all, wait…" Patience is needed for the maturity of your blessings. God does things in His own time. And His own time is the best time. So, relax. Like pregnancy, it must go through the three trimesters to be matured for delivery. So, once you have done all that is needful, release yourself and relax on God for his perfection. Relax, and again I say, RELAX.

CHAPTER 8

UNDERSTANDING COURTSHIP

Once you find or is found, courtship begins. Courtship is the period between when you agree to marry and when you finally get married. It is important to understand that agreeing to marry does not mean MARRIAGE. My father once told me that a lot could happen between the tea cup and the mouth. And this is so true, especially in relationships.

Isaac did not court his wife, but took her into his mother's room same day he met her. However, Jacob courted Racheal for 14 years. So, there is no Biblical prescription on the length of courtship. It could be a few weeks to a few or many years. The length of courtship does not determine the success or failure of a marriage. Be wise.

I believe that there is the need to know the benefits of courtship.

Courtship is a period of discovery. It is a time to discover who you desire or want to marry – his or her temperament, emotions (what makes him/her cry, smile or laugh), likes and dislikes, vision, expectations, culture and beliefs. It is also a time to agree on a number of issues like where to live after marriage, how many children to have, family finances (joint or single accounts), which church to attend (if coming from different denominations), role of in-laws, etc. Maximizing this period of courtship prevents crisis in marriage.

It is important to note that in courtship, everyone pretends. Some pretend deliberately, while others do it unconsciously. In courtship, you accept things that you should naturally reject and refuse, you accommodate behaviors that you do not like and want to stop, you tolerate your partner hoping to earn his/her acceptance.

That is why, everyone should read in-between the lines in courtship as not everything is vocalized. There is a wise saying that not all that glitter is gold! You must hear what is not been said. You must see what is not been shown. And you must discover what is deliberately hidden.

If with all these levels of pretense, there are serious issues in courtship, you should end the relationship no matter how far you have gone. I nearly ended my courtship with my wife after the traditional marriage because of what I saw as ingratitude. Take extra step to discover your partner.

There are behaviors that can negatively affect marriages and the ones that can build them up. Courtship is about attempting to decode a partner and decide whether to marry that particular person or not. It is a period when you try to understand your partner and his/her expectations in marriage.

For instance, there are behaviors that can encourage a partner to show more love or otherwise. There is a thin line between love and infatuation and one cannot know the difference without a discerning spirit especially since there is much pretense in courtship.

Love comes in different guises and people interpret it to benefit their selfishness. My friend, Chisom Anukam, Said, (and I agree), "I believe anybody who thinks about the partner often and misses him/her when he/she is not around, who gets deeper and deeper in looking for ways and means to make the relationship stronger, who at a point is scared to go on and whose intentions are pure and feelings so strong that he/she cannot turn away must be in love. On the other hand, any man who thinks of nothing else about his partner other than the urge to take him or her to bed or the lady only considers how much the man's pocket weighs is not in love."

Failed marriage starts at courtship. Get it right in courtship and enjoy marital bliss. What are the issues that may hinder your progress in courtship (forgive any repetition from Enemies of Marital Bliss – it is for emphasis)?

1. **Past relationships.** People tend to stay connected to past relationships. And if not well managed, this can hinder a blossoming relation. There is

the constant temptation to compare your current partner with your previous partners including your father (for female partners) and mother (for male partners). When you are tempted to compare a current partner with a failed partner, you end up seeing the things you hate. Also, when you compare your partner with a past friend who you care for, but who nonetheless had to move on, you begin to see their shortcomings. Remember that only fools compare. Bible said that they that compare themselves with themselves are not wise. So, avoid comparison. Bury the past. Live in the present, and plan and prepare for the future.

2. **Temperaments**. People have different personality types and this may sometimes be a hindrance to good relationship building. Psychologists and social scientists have told us how these affect relationships. They also postulated on classes that can succeed in building a lasting relationship. But these are just postulations. Marriage is for adults - men and

women – not boys and girls. Men and women are individuals who can control their emotions, manage their temperaments and maintain their calmness even in the face of severe provocations. To succeed, you must tolerate – sometimes nonsense from your partner. But, you must understand the individual differences and appreciate it them. Remember that you cannot marry your replica because like poles repel and opposite poles attract.

3. **Intimate partner violence.** This is a major enemy of relationships, and if this ever occurs in courtships, cut the ship there and then. A partner that physically abuses you in courtship (when you are pretending), will batter you in marriage. It is fallacy to think that he or she will change. Yes, they will change, but not for the better but for the worse. This is because, in marriage, they will see more of the things they do not like, and since you could tolerate their beating in courtship, they will see it as their best tool to correct your 'bad behaviors'. So, run from any partner that

abuses you in courtship. Note that abuse here goes beyond physical to include verbal and emotional abuses. Partners that abuse verbally and emotionally in courtship will do worse including physical abuse in marriage. So, cut the relationship and move on. One may say that a bird in hand is better than twenty in the bush. But what if the bird is dead on arrival or is poisoned? Will you still keep it?

4. **Family relationships**. Although this may not be the case in all situations, I have come to realize that people whose parents had marital challenges are more likely to have marital challenges in their own marriages. Single parents are more likely to give birth to children who will also be single parents. Children from polygamous homes are more likely to marry into polygamous homes, and boys whose fathers had many wives will most likely marry more than one. Children from abusive household will abuse partners and maybe their children too. This is the cycle of evil that must be stopped. So, if you

desire to marry a partner from a heavily abusive home, expect these challenges and have proactive deliberate plans to deal with them. It is not what you wish away. Also, being born again does not necessarily stop it. Expect it and plan for it. If you cannot handle it, walk away. If you desire to continue with the relationship, you should discuss it in courtship and map out plans on how to handle it when it arises. Please do everything not to live in denial.

5. **Respect for parents**. Single partners' love and respect for their parents will reflect on their love and respect for you and your parents. So, a partner who has little or no regards for their parents will most likely have little or no regards for your parents or yourself. So, have this at the back of your mind before saying "I do". A partner who does not respect his or her elders, will not respect yours when he or she comes in contact with them. But a partner that loves and goes the extra mile for parents, elders and other

people (not in pretense), will most likely take good care of you, your parents and elders in marriage. So, watch out for their attitudes. Consciously stimulate discussions on parenting, siblings, the aged, giving, visiting, etc. and gauge the response and physical expressions of your partner.

1. **Giving and receiving**. People are naturally selfish but work to overcome this by choice. Look out for your partner's willingness to give and how they feel when they receive gifts. Selfish people do not become liberal in marriage. Miserly people do not become philanthropic. Do not console yourself by saying, he/she will change. Yes, they will change, but not likely positively. So, discuss this in courtship.

CHAPTER 9

NOW THAT YOU ARE MARRIED

You never know who you married until you are

married. In courtship, everyone pretends

Let me share with you briefly some of the things that have helped us (my wife and I) in the past 19 years to have a peaceful and wonderful marital life. I believe they will help you too as you begin to settle into your marital destiny.

1. **Marriage is an imperfect union of imperfect individuals.** Are we perfect? No. Is our marriage perfect? No. Do we have issues? Yes. Do we solve them without bitterness? Yes. Why? Because we have realized that our union is imperfect, and we too are

imperfect. There is no way two imperfect people can have a perfect relationship. Understanding this makes it easier to accept each other's mistakes, weaknesses and mess which may occur daily, weekly or monthly. But as the years go by, they keep on reducing until you will need to look for them and not find them.

2. **Trust and Confidence in one another.** I travel a lot and so does my wife. We have several phone lines and make hundreds of calls regularly. Not once have we had any reason to suspect each other. Why? Trust and openness. One of my students was worried when I made a statement that expressed our trust. He said to me, "you can only say that if you carry your wife in your bag everywhere you go!" I do not need to carry her in my bag everywhere I go to trust her. Trust is an attitude. It is a choice. I choose to trust my wife. Will you make a similar decision today?

Actually, I carry her around but not in my bag – in my heart. I also carry something more than my wife around (she too carries the same) – GOD. Trust is a basic requirement for marital bliss. There is no love without trust. Therefore, from day one, build trust and confidence in each other.

3. **Open door policy:** Be fully open one to another. Have no secrets. Let everything be done in the open. When you begin to hide information from each other, you are building a wall that may in the future separate you two.

Share common bed, common toilet, common meals and common jokes. These may initially be uncomfortable and sometimes outrightly disgusting, but keep to it. Keep your finances clean and open. Let there be no hidden agenda.

Be open in all things. We live as mentors to both old and young couples (and singles). This position has strengthened us and given us more responsibility which has helped cement our relationship and assisted us in becoming exemplary in marital relationships and child upbringing (we keep working on this).

4. **Daily family prayer.** We started this long before we got married. We began Wednesday prayers while our Church was having weekday services on Tuesdays and Thursdays.

"They that seek me early shall find me". Seek Him early in the morning and commit all the day's activities to Him. Also, offer unto Him the evening sacrifices of praise and thanksgiving and see Him distinguish your life and marriage. Remember all His '*loving kindnesses*' and praise Him for them (Isaiah 63: 7).

5. **Dependence on the Holy Spirit:** We recognized early in our relationship that by strength shall no man prevail (I Sam 2:9); that marital blissful race is not to the swift or to the strong. We depended

and relied completely on the directives of the Holy Spirit. Zach 4:6

Then he answered and spake unto me, saying, This is the word of the LORD unto Zerubbabel, saying, Not by might, nor by power, but by my spirit, saith the LORD of hosts.

6. **Mutual love for God.** This is our greatest assets. We Love God. We fear God. We work for and with God. We reverence Him. We live for Him. This is our lifestyle. Actually, I am a fanatic for CHRIST.

After measuring the impact of this singular point, I concluded by saying, "Do not marry a man that only loves you; rather marry a man that loves God." Do you know why? If he loves God, then based on God's commandment, he must love you. Your love for God will endear you to each other. But if you marry a man that loves you, he may soon stop loving you without any checks in his conscience. We love God. Why? Deuteronomy 10:12

151

And now, Israel, what doth the LORD thy God require of thee, but to fear the LORD thy God, to walk in all his ways, and to love him, and to serve the LORD thy God with all thy heart and with all thy soul,

God bless you so good, and see you at the top. You are too favoured to fail. Enjoy GOD.

As we close this book:

It will be a waste of time and energy for anyone to walk through life without the keeper of life. It is a mere wish to desire to have a good marriage without the author of marriage. Life is not safe except it is saved. Without Christ, crises are sure.

If you know that you are not born again (or you were, but missed it), then you are the one I am talking to right now. You have read this book to this point. It is a proof that you love God, and that you desire to have the best in life. Now obey these simple four (4) instructions and enjoy the best that God has for you:

1. **Understand that you cannot help yourself.** You need God. Therefore, say with me: *"Lord Jesus, I need You. I understand that I cannot save or help myself. I believe that You came, suffered and died on the cross to set me free from sin and Satan. I confess You as my Lord and Personal Saviour. Cancel my name from the book of death; write my name into Your book of life. From today, I make a promise to serve You for the rest of my life. Now I know, I am born again, old things have passed away, and all things have become new. Thank You Lord Jesus for saving me. I am forever grateful in Jesus name."* Amen.

2. **Accept that Jesus has just saved you** (if you truly prayed the above prayer from your heart) and that your sins are forgiven and you are now a new creature, old things have passed away; all things have become new. Congratulations!

3. **Find a Bible believing Church and join.** If you are already in one, stay there and let members bear witness that you are a changed person. If you are not in one, look for one immediately. You need spiritual food to grow in your new faith. You need guidance to stay committed. So, attend the believers foundation and member classes. Learn to trust and walk with God. Get baptized in water and with the Holy Spirit. Join a Service Unit and serve God in spirit and in truth. You will be amazed how fulfilled you will be.

4. **Write me and share your testimony.** We have a gift for you. If truly you read this book, write to me and let me share in your joy and testimony. I am praying for you and I know it will happen soon. God will surely visit you. When He does, write me under the heading: COVENANT EXPERIENCES to <u>droleribe@yahoo. com</u> or P.O. Box 200 PSIN Dutse, Abuja FCT Nigeria, 901101 or call +234 803 547 3223

God bless you.

QUESTIONS AND COMMENTS FROM 1ST EDITION

Questions/Comments:

But Pastor, you guys still have three celebration of marriage? But why? Is traditional one still there? When I went through the book last night, I could not understand as I know there is no traditional stuff in Christian.

SJ

Response

Dear SJ,

Thank you for reading the book. **Marriage is not a passing phase but a settling phase**. It must be done with due diligence.

In the Bible, when Abraham needed a wife for his son Isaac, he sent his servant and the bible records that he paid the family with precious stones - gold, silver, etc. before living with her (Gen 4:53, 56). Jacob also paid 14 years of service to marry his wives (Gen 29:20,27-30). Boaz paid for Ruth (Ruth 4:8-10)

Traditional marriage is not, therefore, **unbiblical**. Every marriage should receive parental blessings. What I stand against is using things that are not biblical or precious for the process such as bowing down to idols, pouring libation to traditional gods, etc. **But traditional marriage is a must**.

Court or Registry wedding gives the woman a legal right to her husband and his property. In Africa, women are denied their rights at the death of their husbands. The Bible requests every man to take care of their family and anyone that fails to do this is seen as an infidel (1 Timothy 5:8). To avoid this, we deliberately go to the court as the court marriage gives a woman the needed legal backing in case of the death of her husband. Also, as the church is focused on wedding and is hardly involved in divorce, we encourage couples to wed in court in case issues arise that will need legal management.

Finally, marriage is of God and must commence, continue, and be completed by God. Starting, therefore, without God is seeking for crisis in disguise. So, until God blesses the marriage, the family has not yet begun. This may be part of the reasons we have issues in Africa, especially in communities where young girls move in to live with men who have made no real commitment to them. This is a recipe for crisis.

Traditional marriage allows the couple to get parental blessings and permission to marry. It also announces to the world that they are about to get married. The court gives the woman a legal backing for leaving her father and joining her husband. But the Church wedding brings down God's presence and blessings; and concretizes the wedding. All are, therefore, important and should be respected and honored. I did the three on February 18, April 12 and April 28, in the year 2000 respectively.

Finally, by the time a young couple goes through these, they are sure of what they want, they have solved problems together and are more aware of their strengths and weaknesses, and they have the support of all.

My final comment is that these need not be expensive. It all depends on how much you have and how much you want to spend. The practice of begging for donation is not biblical and should be stopped. I have a belief that this maybe part of the issues we have that we need to solve.

May my good LORD continue to bless you now and always,

Question/Comments:

I would like to take this opportunity to say a big thank you for the book titled Repositioning for Marital Success. Truly, I have learned how to reposition myself for marriage. I am so expectant and hope has risen inside me

Thank you so much for talking about age issue. I am saying this because I always get men who are younger than me. And this has really made me think maybe there is something wrong somewhere, but now I know age is not an issue anymore

God bless you abundantly

EM

Question/Comments

Greetings in the name of our Lord JESUS!

My name is FFZ from Living Faith Church-Dar es salaam. I thank God who gave me an opportunity to read your book titled "REPOSITIONING FOR MARITAL SUCCESS". I am very blessed with what is inside the Book. The book just opened my understanding when you said that, I have to position myself so as to be located and get married, not only praying and fasting and doing other kingdom responsibilities.

Well, I remember you and your beautiful wife and Children very well and one day you gave us a lift from Our church (WINNERS CHAPEL BANANA) to Kinondoni since we are living at that area till date. I just bought this book last Sunday and started reading it. I am really very blessed by this book. One thing important is that please continue to pray for us because especially for myself, I really need God to intervene in my situation because I am still believing God for a life partner.

…. I have been believing God for a life partner Husband). Several disappointments occurred but yet am striving to secure my marital destiny… I have faith that God who did it to you will also do to me because God is no respecter of persons but a respecter of COVENANTS.

Please continue to pray for me and also if you have released other books, I would love to know so that I can get a copy.

Be blessed!

CN

Printed in the United States
By Bookmasters